Embroidery Machine
ESSENTIALS

How to Stabilize, Hoop and Stitch Decorative Designs

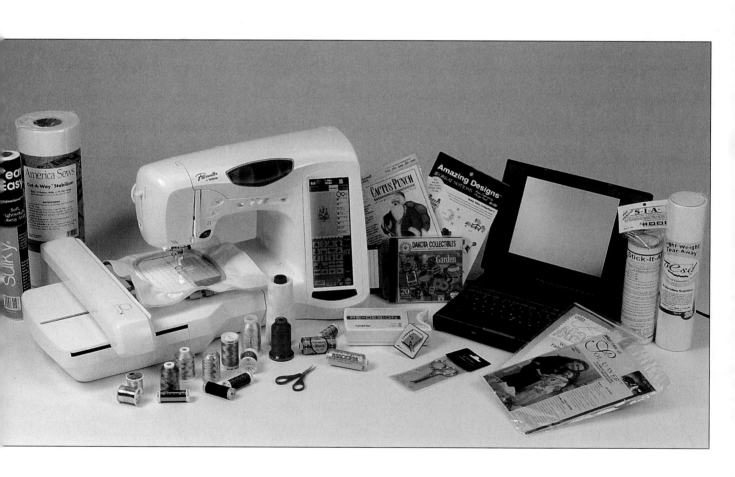

Jeanine Twigg

with Foreword by Lindee Goodall

Published by

krause publications

700 East State Street • Iola, WI 54990-0001
715/445-2214 • FAX: 715/445-4087   www.krause.com

Please call or write for our free catalog of publications. Our toll-free number to place an order or obtain a free catalog is 800-258-0929 or please use our regular business telephone 715-445-2214 for editorial comment and further information.

Library of Congress Cataloging-in-Publication Data

Twigg, Jeanine.
   Embroidery machine essentials. How to stabilize, hoop and stitch decorative designs / Jeanine Twigg; with a forward by Lindee Goodall–1st ed.
      144 p. : col. ill.; 28 cm. + 1 computer optical disc (4 3/4 in.)
Includes index.
ISBN-13: 978-0-87341-999-4
1.   Embroidery, Machine. I. Title
TT772.T93 2001
746.44/028–dc21   00111287

Printed in China.

12 11 10 09 08   12 11 10 9 8

Table of Contents

Chapter 1—
Embroidery Equipment

Baby Lock® design.

Chapter 2—
Embroidery Products

Butterfly designs on pages 4 and 5 from Baby Lock.

Chapter 4—
Creative Embroidery Techniques

Chapter 5—
Embroidery Projects

Chapter 6—
Inspirational Embroidery
Showcase 98

How to Embroider Step-by-step

1. Select a design suitable for the project.

2. Select an appropriate stabilizer for the project fabric. Cut a piece of stabilizer larger than the size of the hoop.

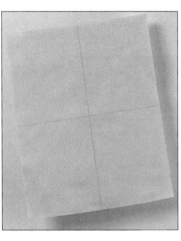

3. Mark the placement of the design on the fabric with a temporary marking pen or pencil.

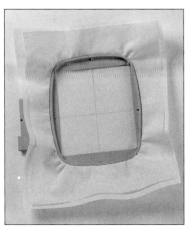

4. Hoop the fabric with the stabilizer. Be sure to align the fabric marking with the notches on the hoop.

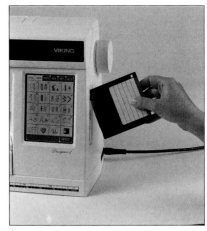

5. Load the design onto the machine.

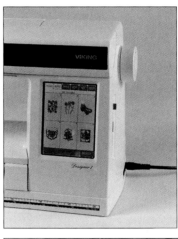

6. Locate and select the design on the machine.

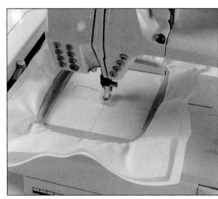

7. Attach the hoop to the embroidery arm. Center the needle directly over the intersecting placement mark.

8. Load the machine with the first color of thread. Start the embroidery process to stitch the first color of the design. When the machine stops, trim any exposed loose threads. Change to the next color thread and restart the machine. Continue until the design is complete. Remove the hoop from the arm of the machine. Trim any loose threads on top of the fabric and clip any bobbin threads within 1/2" from the fabric.

Foreword

by Lindee Goodall, award-winning digitizer and owner of Cactus Punch®, Inc.

"I truly believe that a home embroidery machine is an entertainment device!"

I compare embroidery to baking—if you follow a proven cookie recipe using correct measurements of fresh, quality ingredients, clean equipment and an oven that heats properly, you will get good results. If you start changing the ingredients or proportions the outcome will change. While we don't often think about it, the same principles apply to embroidery. Quality embroidery requires basic skills, quality ingredients, and proper equipment. When you start swapping designs, fabrics, needles, threads, backings and machine tension, you can dramatically alter the end results of an embroidery project.

I didn't know any of this when I got my first embroidery machine. The machine didn't come with lessons and the manual was no help. I learned to use my machine by playing and experimenting—if something didn't work out, I figured out why. Some would call these mistakes; I called them "learning experiences" but never failures.

If I had to list the three primary causes of poor embroidery results, they would be:
- Poor fabric and design combination
- Improper backing choice and poor hooping techniques
- Overly tight thread and bobbin tensions on the machine

Great embroidery is achieved through a good marriage of fabric and design. Not all designs are suitable for all fabrics. Remember, fabrics are made up of thread. By embroidering on it, you are adding more thread. Therefore, ask yourself these questions:

- Can the fabric support the design?
- Does it have enough "breathing room" in its weave to accommodate the design?
- Will the fabric color interfere with the design? (For example, pastel threads are quite translucent and can appear washed out when sewn on intensely colored fabrics.)
- Will the fabric texture negatively affect the design?

The answers to these questions will help you determine if you have the correct fabric and design combination. Be sure to test your design on the same fabric as your project first before embroidering on the real thing.

Hooping an item correctly for embroidery is one of the most important steps of the whole process. It takes attention to detail since poor hooping cannot be corrected after the embroidery process. The hoop needs to be placed in the right position and with the proper tension. And, stabilizers need to be chosen carefully in order to support the design throughout the entire stitching process. For example, a tear-away is not the best choice for knits because of the needle penetrations. If you use a tear-away behind a knit with a design that has fill stitches and running stitches for the outline, your design could become misaligned. Why? The fill stitches perforate the backing compromising its integrity. Without the support of the backing, the fabric can stretch where the backing no longer supports it. When the outlines stitch, the fabric has shifted so the outlines no longer match up with the rest of the design.

Overly tight machine tensions can also cause outline problems (or as I call it, registration problems). You can have interior gaps where fill and satin stitches don't meet correctly. When machine tensions are too tight, they can pull the stitches tighter resulting in narrower satins, pucker the fabric (especially if you use polyester thread), provide poor fabric coverage and even thread and needle breaks. Most embroidery machines set tension automatically—learn how to override them when necessary.

I love embroidery and digitizing because it involves my heart, my head, and my hands. I like it because it always presents new challenges—some of which are creative and others technical.

Jeanine has covered all the basic necessities for producing successful embroidery results. In addition, she's provided step-by-step techniques and projects to lead you down the garden path to beautiful embroidery. Jeanine and I have also teamed up to provide you with some clever embroidery designs. (She designed them and I digitized them.) An embroiderer can never have too many designs! Designs can be reused, taken apart, and recombined for entirely new variations. With the proper combination of skills and supplies, your imagination is truly your only limit!

Albert Einstein said, "Imagination is more important than knowledge." While you do need some knowledge to get started, your imagination will take you the furthest.

When I got my first machine in 1994, there wasn't any information on using home embroidery machines. Today, thanks to Jeanine, you'll have a head start because of the information contained in the pages of this book.

Happy Stitching!

Lindee

Lindee has contributed many hints and tips throughout the book. You can identify her quotes within special purple text boxes like this:

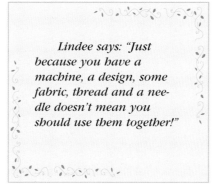

Lindee says: "Just because you have a machine, a design, some fabric, thread and a needle doesn't mean you should use them together!"

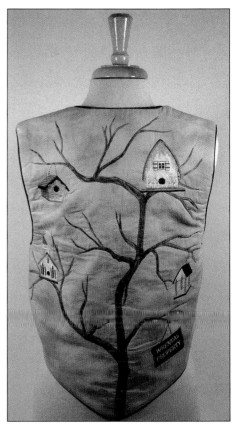

Lindee's creation of handpainted branches with stitched birdhouses. Embroidered logo stitched to lining before sewing vets pieces together. The branches are machine-quilted to hold all the layers together.

Acknowledgments

This book would not be possible without the generosity of the following individuals and companies whose contributions of equipment, threads, stabilizers, accessories, software, designs, stitch-outs and garments fill the pages of this book. As an author and embroidery consumer, I cannot thank you enough for sharing your wonderful products and embroidery talents for inclusion in this book.

For more information on purchasing these and other embroidery products, see the Resources section starting on page 136.

Embroidery Machines and Hardware

Baby Lock
Brother
Elna
Janome

Pfaff
Singer
Viking

Embroidery Thread

American & Efird (Mettler & Signature)
Brother
Coats & Clark
DMC
Fabric Loft/Tristian (Aurifil)
Gutermann
Hoop-It-All
Madeira

OESD (Isacord & Yenmet)
Robison-Anton
Solaractive
Sulky
Superior
Tacony (Crowning Touch)
YLI

Embroidery Stabilizers

Emblematic
Hoop-It-All
HTC
OESD
Pellon

Sew Baby!
Sulky
Tacony (Crowning Touch)
Viking (America Sews)

Baby Lock design.

Embroidery Software/Designs

Amazing Designs (Designs & Software: Letter Pro, Size Express, Smart Sizer)
Baby Lock (Designs)
Buzz Tools (Buzz Tools & Buzz Edit)
Cactus Punch (Designs)
Dakota Collectibles (Designs)
Elna (Designs)
Embroideryarts (Designs)

Hobbyware (Cross Stitch Pattern Maker & Cross-Stitch Clip Art)
Janome (Designs)
Madeira (Color)
OESD (Simple Simon)
Sudberry House (Designs)
Husqvarna/Viking (Designs & Software: ReSize Plus, Cross-Stitcher, Convert & Sort

Embroidery Accessories & Supplies

ABC Embroidery (Embroider's Friend & Snappy)
Cactus Punch (Martha Pullen Thread Stand)
David Textiles (Fabric)
Gingher (scissors)
Hoop-It-All (Hoops and embroidery aids)
Husqvarna/Viking
June Tailor (Thread stand)

Mountainland Manufacturing (Thread Palette)
PD Sixty (Sock Hoopster, Thread Stands)
Peggy's Stitch Eraser
Perfect Hooper (The)
Sew Special
un-do Products

I would also like to thank the following designers who provided garments and accessories for inclusion in this book. These designers are on the cutting edge of embroidery and are taking embroidery onto the next level—an art form. Look for more ideas from these great designers.

Designers

Baby Lock Educators
Carol Bell for Brother International
Nicky Bookout for Bubbles Menagerie
Ann Brodsky for Sew Baby!
Brother Educators
Nancy Cornwell
Linda Crone
Dakota Collectibles
Elna Educators

Embroideryarts
Lindee Goodall
Husqvarna/Viking
Vicki Madigan for Brother International
Linda McGehee
Mary Mulari
Primedia—*Creative Machine Embroidery* magazine
Primedia—*Sew News* magazine

Baby Lock design.

Introduction

The stitching of decorative designs onto fabric using an embroidery machine is a lot like gardening. It takes quality soil, water, seeds, nutrients and sunshine to produce beautiful flowers in a garden. And, it takes quality embroidery equipment, fabric, stabilizers, threads, and needles to produce beautiful designs with an embroidery machine. Both hobbies require time and knowledge before the fruits of your labor can bloom.

This book was designed as a basic guide for use with your embroidery machine. Throughout the book, I offer suggestions to help you achieve successful embroidery results. There are many wonderful products being manufactured to help ensure a fun and easy embroidery experience. When purchasing embroidery products, it is important to remember that every machine stitches with a different outcome. Therefore, choose the brands of products best suited for your machine and your style of decorative embroidery.

The six embroidery designs on the CD have been produced exclusively for this book—you cannot get them anywhere else. I created the designs and Lindee Goodall, the award-winning digitizer and owner of Cactus Punch, personally digitized the designs to perfection. Chapter 5 is dedicated to offer simple projects that you can stitch up using your embroidery machine—including ideas for these exclusive designs. To access the designs, you'll need a computer and the software to use with your brand of embroidery machine. If you're just getting started and don't have the software yet, be sure to substitute the exclusive designs for ones that are on your machine or in your design collection. As a matter of fact, you can use just about any design for these projects—let your imagination be your guide!

As you stitch up your embroidery projects, please pay close attention to these very important tips:

- Be sure to test-stitch designs before starting a project
- Not every design will work on every fabric
- Never copy or share designs with your friends—it is illegal
- Only use quality products designed for use with an embroidery machine
- Always pre-shrink your fabric or garment before stitching
- Use the smallest hoop possible for your design
- Do not use your home embroidery machine for commercial use
- Have your machine tuned-up at least once a year

Look for hundreds of tips just like these in the pages that follow. By the time you're finished reading this book from cover to cover, you'll have the basics to get started on your embroidery adventure. Have fun and be sure to keep *Embroidery Machine Essentials* by your side every step of the way!

Your embroidery friend,

Jeanine

Chapter 1

Embroidery Equipment

Your Machine Choices

When strolling through clothing stores, you'll find stitched embroidery designs on just about everything—from elegant hip-to-floor-embroidered evening gowns to an infant sleeper with a cute little teddy bear on it. These factory-embroidered designs are generated from a computer and stitched onto fabric with high-speed commercial embroidery equipment.

To achieve this look at home, there are two types of machines that can stitch computer generated decorative designs—a home "embroidery only" machine or a home "sewing & embroidery" machine. What's the difference?

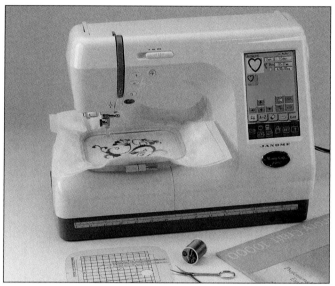

A Janome home "sewing & embroidery" machine.

A Brother® home "embroidery only" machine.

The Home "Embroidery Only" Machine

A home "embroidery only" machine stitches pre-programmed, decorative designs—it does not have the ability to sew standard sewing machine stitches. This type of machine is perfect for those who have a sewing machine and would like to purchase an additional machine for embroidery. It is also perfect for a crafter who does not sew, yet wants to embroider on purchased items or garments.

The Home "Sewing and Embroidery" Machine

With the advancement of technology, electronic home sewing machines can be purchased with on-board embroidery capabilities, an interchangeable embroidery unit or an embroidery accessory that can be purchased separately. A sewing & embroidery machine can be changed from sewing to embroidery by the push of a button or by simply replacing parts of the machine. This all-in-one machine will offer never-ending creative possibilities from sewing to decorative embroidery.

Purchasing Embroidery Equipment and Supplies

All embroidery machines are quality pieces of equipment and are factory tested to ensure stitch perfection. Each machine company has their own brand of equipment with specialty embroidery features and a built-in selection of decorative designs. Some machines feature a built-in computer disk drive where decorative designs can be loaded directly from the computer into the embroidery machine. Others have a slot for a small, machine specific embroidery "card" containing designs that can be loaded directly into the embroidery machine. Then there are some that have both. Some machines hook up directly to the computer, bypassing both methods. Each machine has its own unique qualities from touch screens, to an automatic needle threader, to separate bobbin winders and variable stitch speeds.

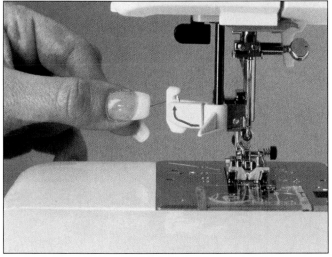

The Janome automatic needle threader.

There are several ways to purchase embroidery equipment and supplies—a local sewing machine dealer, over the Internet or by mail order. When purchasing embroidery equipment and supplies from a local dealer, warranty service and support for the embroidery products should be honored. Some dealers even offer embroidery club meetings. These inspirational meetings are hosted by the dealer and will offer the opportunity to talk with other embroidery equipment owners, share creative embroidery ideas and learn about new products.

Should you decide to purchase equipment and supplies from another source, such as the Internet or mail order, keep in mind that the machine support and warranty work will have to be provided by the company from which you purchased the products. Therefore, a local dealer is not obligated to help or service your equipment should assistance be needed. Some local dealers may sell support packages that include warranty service, embroidery club meetings and technical support. Be sure to make arrangements for these services prior to purchasing the equipment or supplies.

The Embroidery Center from Elna & Baby Lock.

Your Embroidery Workspace

The place you embroider can be anywhere from the kitchen table to an entire room dedicated to embroidery. It is important to embroider on a table that does not move or shift during the stitching process. Be sure to keep on-hand the items you use most during the embroidery process.

A Brother commercial embroidery machine.

Beyond the Hobby: Commercial Embroidery Machines

Home embroidery equipment is not designed for use in a high-volume business. If a home embroidery machine is being used in a business that keeps the machine running for hours at a time, the purchase of commercial embroidery equipment is necessary. A high-speed commercial machine can stitch much faster than conventional home units thus saving the wear on a home unit. In addition, a commercial machine can stitch larger designs and stitch multiple colors without changing threads at each color stop. Embroidery supplies are also available in larger quantities to provide added cost savings for a business.

An assortment of embroidery supplies available in larger, more economical sizes from Pellon, Emblematic, Robison-Anton, and Madeira.

Sue Hausmann, vice president of education at Viking Sewing Machines Inc. and Host of America Sews says: "When selecting an embroidery design, keep in mind on what fabric type and weight it will be embroidered. A very heavy design with high stitch count will weigh down a lightweight knit or woven or sheer. Save these designs for more stable fabrics and choose more open "airy" designs with lower stitch counts. When in doubt, try the design on a scrap of fabric first. You can always make the test design into an accessory, small handbag, glasses case, etc. or incorporate it into a crazy quilt or patchwork project. For the best embroidery stitch on all fabrics invest in good quality thread and embroidery needles.

Your Design Choices

Designs from Amazing Designs, Baby Lock, Dakota Collectibles, Janome, Elna, Cactus Punch, Viking, Brother, Sudberry House and Embroideryarts.

You'll be amazed at the thousands of decorative designs that are available in addition to the built-in or standard designs included with your machine. Look for additional designs at local embroidery machine dealers, independent professional digitizing companies, companies on the Internet and mail order sources.

The Role of the Computer

Here comes the big question—do you need a computer to use with an embroidery machine? Technically, no, but if you want to experience all the design capabilities your embroidery machine has to offer then the answer is yes.

The commercial embroidery industry uses computers to create decorative designs for clothing in the stores. At home, a computer is used in a similar manner. With the aid of brand specific software, a computer can assist you in creating designs, cataloging designs, changing designs, and using designs by professional independent digitizing companies. In addition, the Internet has a vast assortment of free designs that can be downloaded directly to your computer and then stitched using your embroidery equipment.

Vicki Madigan, education consultant for Brother International, says: "If you are new to the world of computing, many local recreation departments, junior colleges and adult continuing education departments offer classes on the Introduction to Personal Computers and Windows (a PC's operating system). Taking the first step in learning the computing basics will help the introductory embroidery machine guide classes go smoother!"

If you do not have a computer, you'll be limited to the use of decorative designs "cards" or "disks" specific for your brand of embroidery machine. The changing or combining of designs is limited to the capabilities of the machine's touch-screen and onboard computer.

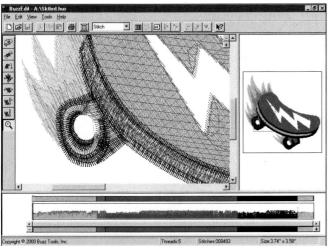

Example of a digitized design from Cactus Punch in the Buzz Tools software.

What Is Digitizing?

Digitizing is the method used to program stitches in a specific order to form an embroidery design. Every design that an embroidery machine stitches has been digitized using a computer.

There are professional digitizing companies, including embroidery machine manufacturers that have trained specialists with artistic skills to paint with thread. These trained specialists, with the aid of high-tech computer software, manipulate the stitches to form digitized decorative designs. These designs are put through a battery of tests before they are packaged and available for sale. Hundreds of hours are spent on designs to ensure a quality product. If a design does not stitch onto a project correctly, first look at the method of hooping (stabilizers, needle, etc.) before contacting the design manufacturer.

With the software available, you can also digitize your own designs (See software choices on page 18). Or, if you have a special design that you would like digitized, "custom digitizing" is available for a fee through independent professional digitizing companies. Custom digitizing is commonly used throughout commercial embroidery businesses and is available for personal use as well.

An example of a computer "disk" and memory card from Viking and Baby Lock.

Embroidery "Card" Versus "Disk"

There are two forms of media in which a design can be purchased for an embroidery machine. The first is a small machine specific memory card that fits directly into the embroidery machine. The embroidery machine's on-board computer locates the designs on the card and will display the designs on the touch-screen. If an embroidery machine accepts cards, be sure to look for designs on brand specific cards.

The second is a computer disk that fits directly into the embroidery machine or computer. Some companies have a built-in disk drive that the on-board computer uses to display designs on the touch-screen of the machine. If your embroidery machine accepts disks, be sure to look for designs on brand specific disks.

Design disks from Cactus Punch, Amazing Designs, Sudberry House, and Dakota Collectibles.

Designs from professional independent digitizing companies come packaged on a computer disk or CD with multiple machine formats. Most companies package theme packs that include anywhere from 5 to 30+ designs per disk. Load the designs onto a computer and then transfer the designs directly to the embroidery machine or onto a disk or card.

Copyright Laws

First, and foremost, it is illegal to sell, trade, share or copy embroidery designs or software. If you are caught, you will be prosecuted. Your home will be raided, equipment confiscated, and incarceration is a possibility.

Second, be fair to those who spend a lot of time and money to develop, create, test, and package designs and software for sale. The companies or individuals who develop, design, and create designs and software legally own the copyrights to the designs.

Example of licensed designs from Elna®, Amazing Designs®, and Janome®.

When purchasing a design, you are buying permission to stitch the designs or use the software for your personal use. This law does not allow you to sell, trade, share, or copy the designs or software without written permission from the company who holds the copyright.

When purchasing a design pack that includes licensed designs of characters such as Mickey Mouse, these designs are for your personal use only. It is illegal to embroider and then sell an item that has been stitched with a licensed design. Not all licensed designs are cartoon characters. Be sure look for the licensed symbol on the outside of the design disk packaging before making a purchase.

The same copyright law governs free designs. Some companies offer free designs that can be downloaded onto a computer and tested for digitizing quality. Companies that offer free designs hope you'll purchase more once you try their test designs. Look for free test designs on the Internet at the Web sites of professional digitizing companies.

Example of a high stitch count, dense design from Cactus Punch.

Choosing Designs

There are no limits to the creativity in stitching embroidery designs. With so many designs available, how do you choose? For best results, select embroidery designs from a reputable digitizing company, such as embroidery machine manufacturers or professional independent digitizing companies.

Everyone's taste in decorative designs is different. Choose designs based on the weight and type of fabric. Choose open and airy designs for lightweight fabrics and larger dense designs for heavier fabrics. Select designs from reputable companies that produce consistent quality designs. It is important to remember that not every design will stitch on every fabric. And, not all fabrics are appropriate for embroidery.

Stitch Counts

Each digitized design has a number that is associated with the size of the design. This number represents the number of stitches in the design. A higher number could indicate that the design is large or dense. A lower number could indicate that the design is small or airy. This number is important when it comes to choosing the stabilizer for the fabric. (See more on stabilizing choices starting on page 21.)

Design Sizes

Digitized designs come in various sizes. However, the standard size of a design for home embroidery fits into the parameters of a 4" x 4" hoop area. Many companies provide sizes for their designs in metric or inches. If you have a design that is sized in centimeters, multiply the size by .3937 to determine the size in inches. If you have a design that is sized in millimeters, multiply the size by .03937 to determine the size in inches. You can also determine how dense a design is by the size. If a design has a large stitch count and is small in size, it is considered to be a dense design. The best way to determine the actual size and density of a design is to first test-stitch the design. (See more about test-stitching designs on page 48.) If a machine specific design comes with approximate minutes of stitching time, keep in mind that this indicates actual stitching time. Be sure to add more time for the changing and trimming of threads.

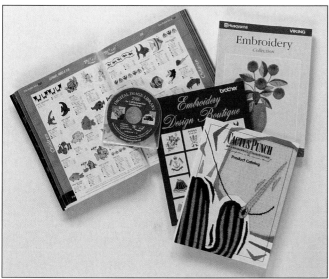

Stock design catalogs from OESD, Viking, Brother, and Cactus Punch.

Stock Designs

Designs that are ready-made and available for purchase are called "stock designs". Stock designs can be purchased from a local embroidery machine dealer, independent professional digitizing companies, the Internet, or mail order companies. Look for design packs that offer multiple designs with a theme. Most designs are digitized to fit within a 4" x 4" standard hoop area unless otherwise noted.

Stock designs can be purchased individually from companies on the Internet. Be sure to purchase quality, digitized designs from reputable companies. The designs are transferred from the selling company directly to a computer via the Internet. Designs can be sold individually or in a multi-design theme pack.

Amateur Design Digitizers

If you decide to download designs off the Internet from an amateur design digitizer or an unknown source, it is very important to test-stitch the design (see page 48) in order to verify the stitch quality. Be sure to have up-to-date virus scanning software on your computer to detect viruses that may be attached to designs from unknown sources.

Educational Material

Most embroidery supply manufacturers provide instructions on how to use their equipment, software, and accessories. Look for educational material in the following locations:

- Videos that come packaged with the embroidery equipment, software, or accessories
- The touch-screen on embroidery machines
- The instructional manual that comes with your machine
- The "Help" section of your product specific software programs
- The PDF (portable document format) files on design disks
- Company Web sites on the Internet

PDF files on a disk often contain updated or enhanced information that is not available in the user's manual. The Adobe Acrobat Reader software can read this type of file. It is advisable to print, download, or read the information contained in a PDF file. Some software programs and design disks do not come with user's manuals only viewable PDF files.

Internet Embroidery Web Sites

The Internet is a valuable resource for you. Just about every company that sells or manufactures embroidery equipment and supplies has a Web site that is designed to provide you with up-to-date information on products, project ideas and embroidery tips. There are even groups that chat online about embroidery. You'll be amazed at the wealth of information found on the Internet. (See Resources starting on page 136.)

Your Software Choices

There are many different types of software available for creating and manipulating embroidery designs. As technology continues to advance, look for new and current versions of software available for your brand of embroidery equipment.

Cross-stitch software from Hobby Ware and Viking.

Editing Software

This type of software is designed to manipulate and change the stitches of digitized designs. From the editing of jump stitches to the combining of large designs to stitch in color sequences, it works as a full-featured stitch editor. Import a design into the software, make changes and save it to the proper format for your machine specific software.

Customizing Software

This type of software will assist in the combining of digitized designs. From adding letters or words to combining designs, this software works as a design customizer. Once the changes are made you can download the designs directly to the embroidery machine or onto a machine specific card or disk.

Sizing, editing, and professional software from Viking, Buzz Tools, Amazing Designs, and OESD.

Digitizing Software

This type of software will assist you in creating your own designs. Scan images into the software; create designs using a paint program on the computer or use clipart from other computer software packages for digitizing. Consider learning the basics of digitizing to become familiar with the entire embroidery process. Be patient, as it takes a lot of practice to learn the art of digitizing.

Cross-stitch Software

If you love the look of cross-stitch but do not have time to stitch the designs by hand, then this type of software is for you. Scan in designs, chart original designs, and choose from a large stock of ready-made designs. The software will assist in creating cross-stitch designs that can be stitched on an embroidery machine.

Sizing Software

This type of software will enlarge or reduce designs without changing the integrity of the original design. Sometimes when changing the size of a design directly on an embroidery machine, the stitch density changes, too. The stitches may be too tight when reduced and more spread apart when enlarged. The software will compensate for the stitch count as it reduces or enlarges the design.

Colorizing, lettering, and design management software from Madeira®, Amazing Designs®, Buzz Tools®, and Viking.

Colorizing Software

This type of software aids in the selecting of colors for designs and can provide an accurate representation of a stitched design on fabric. The programs will also include the color names and numbers of threads from one or more major thread companies and assist with color number conversions between the thread brands.

Cataloging Software

This type of software assists with the organizing of designs, the format conversion of designs and the printing of designs for template making. It searches for embroidery design formats on the hard drive of a computer and displays the designs on the screen. Simply select a design and the software opens the design directly into the proper software for your embroidery equipment.

Lettering Software

Packed with a large selection of font sizes and styles, this type of software assists in adding words and letters to embroidery designs.

Design Transfer Equipment Choices

After making, changing, or editing designs on the computer, the designs will need to be transferred to the embroidery machine for stitching with the aid of a cable, read/writer box, computer disk, or PC Card. The process of transferring from a computer to the embroidery machine is called "downloading". The process of transferring from the embroidery machine to a computer is called "uploading". Both processes are achieved by using a piece of interface equipment between the computer and the embroidery machine.

design and then download the designs to a machine specific blank card.

Design transfer from a computer disk to a Viking embroidery machine.

Computer Disk

Some embroidery machines have a slot that accepts a computer disk. Load, install, and make changes to designs on a computer through the appropriate computer software and then download the designs onto a computer disk for stitching on embroidery equipment. A computer disk allows the transfer of designs when the embroidery equipment and computer equipment are in two separate rooms.

Design transfer of Sudberry designs through the Baby Lock card read/writer box.

Card Read/Writer Box

Some machines use the computer to transfer designs to and from the embroidery machine through a card read/writer box. A card read/writer box will allow the transfer of designs from the computer directly to a machine specific "blank card" that can be inserted into the embroidery machine.

In addition, the contents of a card can be transferred to the computer. Once the designs are on the computer, make the desired enhancements to the

Design transfer through a direct connection from the computer to the Janome embroidery machine.

Direct Connect

With the aid of a cable, some embroidery machines can have a direct hookup from the computer to the embroidery machine. This process makes downloading and uploading a breeze. Use the computer to load, install, or make changes to designs and simply transfer the designs into the memory of the embroidery equipment. This process will require the computer to be close to the embroidery machine, which makes a laptop computer ideal for this type of connection.

PC Card

A PC Card has a much higher storage capacity and is available for use with some embroidery machines. This same technology is used to transfer digital camera photographs from the camera to the computer. Some laptop computers have a PC Card slot on the side of the machine, but desktop computers will require an external read/writer device. A PC card allows the transfer of designs when the embroidery equipment and computer equipment are in two separate rooms.

Embroidery Formats

Every embroidery machine has a file extension associated with a design. For example, a Brother embroidery machine recognizes a design with the extension .pes (flower.pes). Be sure the design is in the correct format before transferring designs to the embroidery equipment. When purchasing designs from professional digitizing companies, be sure to load or install designs in the correct format for the embroidery equipment. Prior to purchasing designs, be sure the designs on the disk are for your machine format.

.csd - POEM, Huskygram and Singer EU
.dst - Tajima
.exp - DOS expanded
.hus - Husqvarna/Viking
.pcs - PC Pfaff
.pes - Baby Lock, Bernina® Deco, Brother
.sew - Janome, Elna, Kenmore, Bernina
.shv - Viking Designer 1
.xxx - Singer SL1000
.jcf - Janome 10000

> *Lindee says: "There are no extensions listed for MacIntosh since this type of format does not need them. You may find Mac Pfaff files with a ".pcm" or a ".pcmac" appended to their names."*

Chapter 2

Embroidery Products

 hen it comes to supplies for the embroidery process, there are certain products that are necessary to help embroider decorative designs successfully. The right combination of embroidery products will make the difference in the appearance of the finished product.

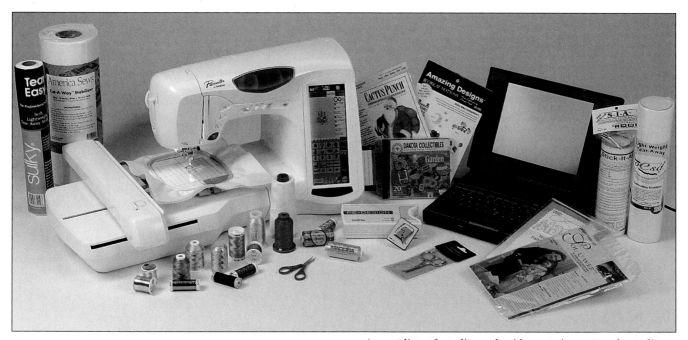

A sampling of quality embroidery equipment and supplies.

Your Stabilizer Choices

A stabilizer is the foundation for a decorative design. The purpose of a stabilizer is to hold the fabric as the embroidery machine forms a secure stitch. If the fabric is not stabilized correctly, the project could become warped, puckered, or ruined. Use a stabilizer that does not stretch in any direction—up/down, left/right, or corner to corner. If the stabilizer stretches, it will fail to stabilize the fabric, which could result in a poorly stitched design.

It is important to match the stabilizer with the weight and type of the fabric. As a general rule—if the fabric stretches, use a cut-away stabilizer, if it doesn't, use a tear-away stabilizer. Too heavy of a stabilizer on lightweight fabric will make the embroidery stiff. Too light of a stabilizer on heavyweight fabric can warp a design. Choose stabilizers based on the drape of the fabric used in the project.

An assortment of stabilizers from Sulky®, OESD, HTC, Pellon®, Hoop-It-All®, Tacony, Viking and YLI.

For example, a lightweight fabric requires a light-weight stabilizer.

Stabilizers should not interfere with the design or the fabric. They are used to support the stitches on the fabric. Purchase stabilizers based on perform-ance, not price. The more stitches the design has the more backing you will need. Find the right combina-tion and be sure to test your designs first.

> *Lindee says: "If you've ever had an outline separate from the rest of your design, the culprit is most often the backing. When using a tear-away for large areas of fills, stitches can perfo-rate the backing causing it to lose stability, which allows the fabric to stretch. If you are using a professionally digitized design or having prob-lems with the outlines, try using a cut-away stabi-lizer."*

Starter packages of stabilizers.

When using stabilizers in the Test-Stitch Process (see page 131), purchase small packages of stabiliz-ers. Some companies sell stabilizer starter kits or small packages of stabilizers for testing purposes. Once a preference for certain stabilizer brands has been identified, purchase the ones you like best in large quantities on rolls in various lengths and widths. Purchasing on rolls can offer cost savings and the convenience of cutting the stabilizer for the vari-ous hoop sizes. Some companies even offer pre-cut stabilizer pieces that are a time saver for certain hoop sizes.

There are only rare occasions when a stabilizer would not be used. Stabilizers are not required when stitching some dimensional embroidery on organza or organdy (see page 61) and when texturizing Polarfleece® (see page 67). Be sure to test your inno-vative ideas on practice material before starting the project.

> *Lisa Shepard, designer and author of the book* African Accents, *says: "There are times when your fusible interfacing can double as embroi-dery backing. For example, when you apply fusible interfacing to a jacket lapel facing, this often gives just enough stability to embellish with embroidery. As always, make a sample that duplicates all of the layers involved and test the stitches before you embroider the actual gar-ment."*

Topping

This is the term given to stabilizers that are used on top of the fabric. They can be hooped with the fabric or secured to the fabric with a spray adhesive. Toppings are made of either a water-soluble or per-manent vinyl material that hold down the nap of the fabric to prevent the threads from becoming imbed-ded into the loft of the fibers.

Backing

This is the term given to stabilizers that are used on the backside of the fabric. The appropriate back-ing will prolong the life of the embroidery and sup-port the garment as the design is stitched to the fab-ric. A backing will also reduce the friction between the fabric and the needle as the machine is stitching. The stabilizer will absorb the heat of the needle to keep the fabric a constant temperature during the stitching process. At times, it may be necessary to combine different stabilizers in the same project.

Sometimes it is best to add two layers of a light-weight backing rather than one heavier weight. Trim the two layers at different levels to help the backing lay flat. If more than one layer of backing is needed, hoop one layer with the fabric and attach the second layer with spray adhesive on the backside of the hooped fabric. The correct backing will improve the stitch quality of a design.

> *"Depending on the project, select a stabilizer that can be placed in the hoop, under the hoop, or stuck to the hoop; it can be ironed on, pinned in place, or adhered with a spray adhesive. You'll know when you have the right stabilizer when the stitches lie perfectly without sinking into the fabric. The design or project is positioned perfectly when the fabric doesn't slip during the stitching process and the stitched project doesn't sag, pull, or pucker." —Sulky Book #900B11,* Sulky Secrets to Successful Stabilizing.

Water-soluble

This type of stabilizer disintegrates when it comes in contact with water. In its original state, it is a see-through stabilizer that is mostly used as a topping to hold down the fabric's fibers during the embroidery process. Either hoop this stabilizer with the fabric or use a spray adhesive to secure it to the top of the fabric. After stitching a design, the stabilizer is torn away from the motif and discarded. Use a sponge to lightly dab the fabric to remove the stabilizer that may be lodged in between the stitching.

A heavyweight, water-soluble stabilizer is perfect for making lace and dimensional designs. After stitching the design, rinse the motif in warm water until the stabilizer disappears. Some brands of water-soluble stabilizers should be kept in airtight containers to prevent them from drying out and becoming brittle due to air exposure. Use a water-soluble topping for designs that are spacious and have numerous jump stitches. It helps keep the jump stitch threads on top of the stabilizer for trimming ease after the embroidery process.

Cut-away

This type of stabilizer is cut away after the stitching process. It is used on the backside of a design and is available in several different weights. After embroidering the design, trim all but 1/4" from the stabilizer on the backside of the project. Be sure to keep the stabilizer and fabric visible while cutting away the stabilizer. Round the corners and be careful not to cut your project.

Cut-away stabilizers are perfect for unstable fabrics such as knits, denim, and linen. If the fabric has a tendency to shift while being stitched, then a cut-away stabilizer is recommended. This type of stabilizer continues to support the design after washing and will prevent shrinkage.

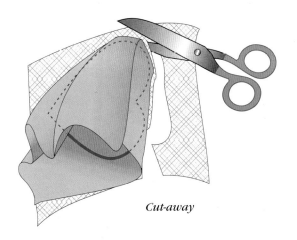

Cut-away

Tear-away

This type of stabilizer is torn away after the stitching process. It is used on the backside of the design and is available in several different weights. This stabilizer is recommended for stable, woven fabrics and should tear away easily in all directions for easy removal. A heavyweight tear-away is used only for heavier weight fabrics that can tolerate a high stitch count design. The fabric must support the weight of the thread and stay secure when the stabilizer is torn away. During the embroidery process the stabilizer is actually separated from the design when the needle penetrates the fabric, which aids in the removal of the stabilizer. It's important to know that tear-away stabilizers will not hold the design area after washing and will dissolve over time through the washing process.

Tear-away stabilizers can pull on threads as they are removed from the embroidered design. Design and fabric distortion can happen when pulling too hard to remove excess stabilizer from the back of the stitched design. The tugs will pull on the threads and distort the design or even harm the fabric. If the stabilizer is hard to remove, cut the stabilizer within 1/4" from the design and allow frequent washings to remove the extra stabilizer surrounding the design.

Tear-away

Adhesive

This type of stabilizer has an adhesive coating on one side that is protected by a removable paper sheet and is available as a cut-away or tear-away stabilizer. There are many different ways to use this stabilizer. The most common is for "hoopless embroidery" (see page 47). Adhesive stabilizers are perfect for fabrics that should not be hooped such as Polarfleece®, velvet, velour, certain knits, and hard-to-hoop areas such as collars and cuffs. Hoop the adhesive stabilizer or secure the stabilizer to the backside of the hoop. An adhesive stabilizer is a form of contact paper. The longer it is left on an item, the harder it is to remove. Therefore, remove the adhesive stabilizer from the surface of hoops directly after the embroidery process. Use a specialty "goo" remover to clean any adhesive residue left on the hoop.

Iron-on

This type of stabilizer has a temporary heat sensitive coating and is available as a cut-away or tear-away. Iron the stabilizer onto the back of the project before the hooping process. It is perfect for stabilizing knits during the hooping and stitching process.

> *Lindee recommends: "When using an iron-on backing on knits, make sure it is a cut-away and not a tear-away. As with any tear-away backing on knits, you may be disappointed with the end results."*

Melt-away

This type of stabilizer is removed from the design with the aid of a household iron after the embroidery process. The fabric must be able to tolerate heat and the iron should be set for polyester fabric. Press the back of the embroidered design until the stabilizer melts into little nuggets that can be brushed away from the fabric. It's amazing—there will be no residue left on your iron.

Iron-away

This type of stabilizer is removed from the design after the embroidery process with the aid of a household iron. Press the back of the embroidered design until the stabilizer becomes black and brittle. Use a fine bristle brush to sweep away the stabilizer from the motif. Do not touch water to the project until the removal of the stabilizer is complete.

Mesh

This type of stabilizer is a translucent cut-away material that is perfect for light-colored fabrics, such as white shirts or sheer blouses. Mesh stabilizers are permanent and will not interfere with the drape of fabrics as they support the embroidery design. This stabilizer tends to stretch and should be used only on stable woven fabric.

Liquid Stabilizer/Spray Starch

Use a liquid stabilizer on fabrics that slip and slide during the hooping process to add support to the weight of the fabric. Brush the liquid stabilizer onto the fabric and allow the fabric to dry. Gently iron to stiffen the fabric and then hoop with the appropriate stabilizer for the fabric.

Spray starch can be used in the same fashion. Spray the starch onto the fabric and press immediately to stiffen the fabric. Be sure to follow manufacturer instructions for best results. It is best when used on natural fibers such as linen and cotton before the hooping process. After the embroidery process, never use spray starch on the right side of the fabric, as it will dull the appearance of the embroidered motif— especially designs stitched with rayon threads.

Spray Adhesives

A can of temporary spray adhesive should always be handy during the embroidery process. You'll be amazed at the many uses for this product. Use a spray adhesive to gently secure a topping/backing to fabric before the hooping process, to spray onto appliqué pieces, or to hold two pieces of embroidery products together. Look for a brand of adhesive that is designed for machine embroidery. Use spray adhesives away from embroidery equipment to prevent the over-spray from touching the machinery. Consider spraying directly into a large empty box to protect the surroundings from the over-spray.

Be sure to shake the can well before use and spray in a well-ventilated area. Clean the surrounding area with soap and water. Do not spray the garment to be stitched—spray the stabilizer or appliqué only. Some spray adhesives dissipate from the fabric within 24-48 hours.

> *Lindee says: "Use a spray adhesive immediately before the stitching process. The spray can dissipate quickly depending on the brand and humidity ."*

Foam

Using a piece of embroidery foam as a topping can offer a raised embroidered effect on fabric. Foam is sold in several different colors and thicknesses. Designs should be digitized specially for use with foam and are usually simple satin-stitched designs. Before stitching, cut a piece of foam slightly larger than the design and place it on top of the fabric. The stitches will cover up and cut the foam during the embroidery process, resulting in raised embroidery.

Permanent Color Topping

Permanent vinyl is a topping that can help hide fabric fibers that may show through embroidery stitches. It is great for light-colored threads being stitched onto dark-colored fabrics. Available in an assortment of colors, use the closest coordinating vinyl color to the thread. It is available as a plain or adhesive topping that tears away easily. There is even clear vinyl for toweling, velvet, or any other material that requires the fabric nap to be held down during the embroidery process.

Interfacing

There will be times when it will be necessary to interface an unstable fabric, such as knits, to hold the shape of the fabric prior to the hooping process. Knit fabrics can stretch or warp during the hooping and embroidery process. Choose a lightweight, soft material that will not add bulk to the fabric, such as a fusible tricot interfacing. By fusing a tricot interfacing to the backside of the fabric perpendicular to the stretch of the fabric, the stitching area mimics that of a woven fabric. For a temporary hold, try lightly fusing the interfacing to an area of the fabric larger than the hoop size. After embroidering the project, gently lift up the interfacing and trim with pinking scissors close to the outer edge of the motif. Adding an interfacing will make the difference in the end result without adding bulk to the design.

Charles Arana, director of sales and marketing for Pellon®, says: "Interfacings are sewing and craft aids that shape, support, and stabilize fabrics. For embroidery, it is important to choose a non-wowen stabilizer that does not strech, shrink or ravel and can be washed or dry-cleaned. Also, consider a textured water-soluble stabilizer that is translucent for easy placement since it will not shift during the embroidery process and will disintegrate, when sprayed or washed with water, without leaving a residue or odor."

Your Hoop Choices

The purpose of a hoop is to hold the fabric and stabilizer during the embroidery process. The standard hoops that come with your machine have two parts—an inner and an outer hoop. The outer hoop holds the tension and the inner hoop holds the layers of the fabric and stabilizer together during the embroidery process.

It is extremely important to hoop the fabric taut to prevent shifting during the embroidery process. The screw on the outside of the hoop is used to loosen or tighten the hoop tension depending on the thickness of the fabric and stabilizer. Hoop and unhoop the fabric with the stabilizer to achieve the perfect hoop tension, before securing the pieces in the hoop. It is not advisable to tighten the screw on the hoop once the inner hoop has been set. Use a firm surface when hooping your fabric. When a firm surface is not used, your fabric will not be tight in the hoop and waves of the fabric will be visible on the inside of the hoop. It's best to hoop the fabric with the grain of the fabric to allow the design to stitch and drape on the fabric properly.

Frequently used hoops can stretch over time. Consider replacing your frequently used hoops when

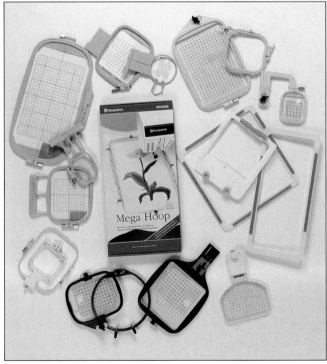

An assortment of hoops from Brother, Baby Lock, PD Sixty, Viking, Elna, Janome, and Hoop-It-All.

you take your machine in for its annual checkup. Use stretched out hoops for heavier weight fabric such as Polarfleece® and denim. Be sure to mark the hoop "old" so as to not confuse it with a new one.

Hoop Sizes

Hoops come in different sizes and shapes that vary with each embroidery machine manufacturer. It is important that designs are stitched in the smallest hoop possible to accommodate the design. If a small design is hooped in a larger hoop, the fabric may shift during the embroidery process and the design will not be aligned properly. Most home embroidery designs are digitized for use within a standard 4" x 4" hoop area unless otherwise stated.

Hoop sizes vary—from mini hoops to giant hoops. It is important that your machine recognizes the size and shape of the hoop being used. Consult the owner's manual on how to set the hoop size on your machine.

Keep in mind that it is more difficult to keep the fabric taut in a larger hoop. If a larger hoop does not hold the fabric well, it may be necessary to secure the materials together with a spray adhesive or a fusible stabilizer to prevent them from shifting in the hoop during the embroidery process.

If the area of a ready-made garment is too small to hoop, open nearby seams carefully to allow more room to hoop the fabric with the stabilizer. Or, for smaller areas, hoop the adhesive stabilizer and pin the object to be stitched onto the adhesive paper.

Hoop Shapes

Hoops come in various shapes and styles. Some hoops are considered standard hoop shapes while others are considered specialty hoop shapes. Each one has a purpose to aid in the hooping process. Consult a local embroidery machine dealer for accessory hoops that are available for your machine. As the size of the embroidery area continues to grow with each new model of machine, look for different hoop sizes and shapes of hoops for embroidery convenience.

Rectangular

Rectangular hoops are the most commonly manufactured shape. The width of the hoop is usually the same, but the length of the hoop varies from 5" to over 18" and varies between each machine manufacturer. The longer the hoop, the more important it is to properly secure the fabric in the hoop.

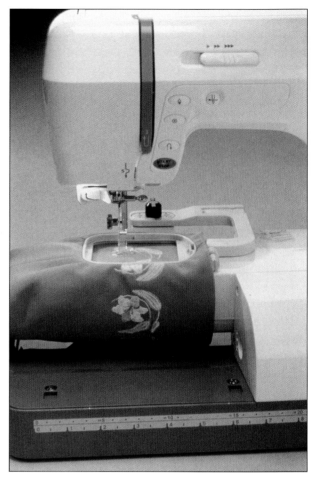

The Janome free-arm hoop for hard-to-hoop small areas.

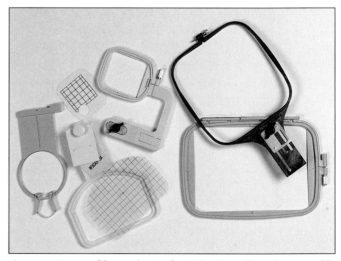

An assortment of hoop shapes from Brother, Elna, Janome, PD Sixty, and Viking.

Circular

There are several types of circular hoops available. Circular hoops with clip-style inner rings are designed for quick hooping with lightweight fabrics. Small circular hoops with the "push-in" inner ring are made for hooping in tight areas or for petite designs.

Frame

A frame hoop does not have an inner ring and is available for the "hoopless" stabilizing of fabric. This unique hoop has only an outer hoop with a flange that holds a piece of adhesive stabilizer. A frame hoop is perfect for hard-to-hoop fabrics and projects, such as velvet, velour, edge embroidery, cuffs of shirts and more. Some frame hoops have a screw-on plate to hold the brim of a cap during the embroidery process.

Specialty

There are specialty hoops available to fit your machine. Look for innovative products that provide stability for hard-to-hoop items such as socks and caps. These hoops fit on nearly every machine and will make the hooping process simple.

Your Needle Choices

A clean, well functioning needle will result in quality, stitched designs. Therefore, changing needles often is the best way to improve your embroidery. Stabilizers can dull needles quickly, which can ultimately affect the machine tension. Choose the smallest needle size for your design, fabric, and thread. The thread should pass through the eye of the needle easily. Needles create the hole for the thread to pass through the fabric. Use a smaller needle for more detailed designs and a larger needle for dense fabrics to penetrate the fabric and prevent thread breakage. When changing threads, clip the thread by the spool and pull the thread through the needle to avoid tension problems.

When changing needles, place an index card over the throat plate of the machine to prevent the needle from slipping into the machine. After stitching a dense design, place a new needle in the machine to stitch the outline. This will ensure a clean finish to the design. To properly dispose of dull needles, store them in an empty film container or a pill bottle. Discard the container when it is full.

Needle Sizes

The smaller the needle, the more detailed the design. A smaller needle will also prevent over penetration of the fabric, which can cause the fabric to weaken underneath the design. A larger needle produces larger holes in fabric and is best used on a dense fabric. A thinner thread should be used with a smaller needle and a thicker thread should be used with a larger needle.

Needles come in sizes that range from 60/8 to 110/18—the larger the number, the larger the needle, with 75/11 or 80/12 being the most standard size. For example, use a size 70/10 sharp for organdy or batiste fabrics and use a 100/16 for dense woven denim. Always test your design with a new needle to

An assortment of needles from Schmetz, Organ, and Madeira.

determine whether the correct needle has been chosen for the project.

> *"It is important to use a 90/14 sewing (sharp or ballpoint), topstitching or embroidery needle with 30-weight rayon, cotton or any metallic threads."*—Sulky Book #900B13, Sulky Secrets to Successful Quilting.

Embroidery

An embroidery needle is the basic needle for most types of machine embroidery. The needle has a slightly larger eye and a slightly rounded tip. It can be used with most standard weight threads.

Sharp

This type of needle is sharp to the touch and will cut through the fabric fibers to form a stitch. Use sharp needles for woven fabrics only. They are available in many sizes, depending on the weight of fabric—for lightweight sheers to heavyweight canvas.

Universal or Ballpoint

Both a universal needle and a ballpoint needle have a rounded tip for penetrating the fabric between the fibers to form a stitch. A ballpoint needle tip is slightly more rounded for knit fabrics. The universal needle is designed for use with both woven and knit fabrics. These needles tend to make larger holes in the fabric. Therefore, consider using a slightly heavier weight of thread and steam the fabric heavily on the backside of the design after the embroidery process.

Metallic

Metallic needles have a larger eye with a grooved shaft that allows the thread to pass through the fabric and needle easily. Metallic needles can prevent overheating and breakage of delicate metal fibers. Needles designed for metallic thread are indicated on the package as such. (See information about metallic threads on page 29.)

Your Thread Choices

Selecting the proper thread for your design is fun, yet challenging. It is critical to choose the right thread for the fabric, as well as for the design to be stitched. Use only threads that are manufactured for high-speed automatic embroidery; regular sewing thread should not be used in an embroidery machine.

> *Lindee recommends: "Using quality embroidery threads is very important to the success of your project. Bargain threads are not a bargain when they continuously shred or break during the embroidery process."*

Threads are available from either two sources—natural or synthetic fibers. Cotton, wool, and rayon are natural threads. Polyester, acrylic and nylon are synthetic fibers. Synthetic threads have more strength but tend to stretch during the embroidery process. Changes in tension may be required when sewing with synthetic threads.

With the advancement in technology, there are many choices of quality threads to make a design radiate with color. From shiny to matte finishes, the number of thread choices and the infinite number of color choices can be overwhelming. It is important to remember to purchase quality products as the thread makes the difference in the end result.

Thread Weight

Threads are available in different weights, which are represented by a number—the lower the number, the thicker the thread. Most designs are digitized for use with a 40-weight rayon thread. Using a thread any size above or below this number may require adjustment to the decorative design. A 30-weight thread is best to use for stitching the outline of a design or in satin stitches to provide better coverage over fabric. Bobbin threads should be 60-weight or higher.

For best results, dense designs should be stitched with a thinner embroidery thread. Tiny embroidery stitches may require a finer thread and fill-in stitches may require a thicker thread. Combining thread weights in a design is a simple way to add dimension.

An assortment of rayon thread from Sulky, Madeira, Gutermann®, Coats & Clark, Robison-Anton, and A&E®.

Rayon

The most popular of embroidery threads, this high-sheen thread provides an elegant finish to projects. Available in 30, 40, and 50 thread weight, this all-natural thread is known for its ability to run smoothly through the embroidery machine. Rayon thread may require a looser machine tension when stitching designs.

For best results, use embroidery needles when stitching with rayon thread and change the needles regularly to prevent stitching problems. Do not use bleach when laundering items stitched with rayon. It is best to wash this type of thread with mild soap or detergent.

An assortment of polyester thread from Sulky, Madeira, Gutermann, OESD (Isacord), A&E (Mettler), and Robison-Anton.

Polyester

This strong, durable synthetic thread is colorfast which makes it perfect for a large variety of applications. Polyester thread is most commonly used on children's wear since it can be bleached without harming the thread. A tighter upper thread tension may be required since this thread tends to stretch during the embroidery process. Polyester thread can be manufactured in neon colors and has a high-tech sheen that is similar to rayon.

An assortment of cotton thread from Mettler, Aurifil, Brother, DMC, Madeira, and Gutermann.

Cotton

Cotton is the thread of choice for a matte finish on embroidered items. Perfect for all aspects of embroidery including heirloom pieces, this wonderful thread is available in the largest range of thread weights, the thinnest being 100-weight and the thick-

est being 30-weight. A lightweight (60) cotton thread can be used in the bobbin, too, for projects that are reversible. Cotton thread, with its natural fiber content, can shrink when not laundered properly. Wash a project in cold water to prevent shrinkage. When pressing the design after the stitching process, do not use steam—the steam could potentially shrink the thread and cause the design to warp. Cotton threads produce more lint in the bobbin case area; therefore, it is best to clean your bobbin housing regularly to avoid the buildup of lint.

An assortment of metallic thread from A&E (Signature, Mettler), Gutermann, Sulky, Superior, and OESD (Yenmet).

Metallic

Metallic threads add a beautiful hint of sparkle to a design. Metallic threads are made from a metal foil wrap covering a strand of thread. The base thread should be made of a strong fiber and the metal should be coated with a sealant to provide a smooth running thread. Look for metallic threads that are smooth when being passed through your thumb and first finger. If they are smooth to the touch, they will run smoothly through the embroidery machine.

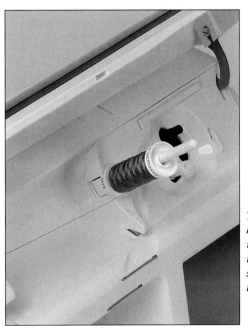

To avoid the kinking of metallic thread, use a vertical spool holder on the machine.

Some designs and fabrics may not be suitable for metallic threads. Use metallic threads in designs with long stitches to add highlights to a design. Short, packed stitches tend to cause kinks in the thread as it pulls off the spool. Avoid using metallic threads for small alphabetic letters and over previous stitching. The previously stitched threads could catch on the metallic thread and cause it to break. Metallic threads tend to kink while unwinding off small, compact spools. If this happens, try using a larger spool of thread, a vertical thread spool holder, or thread nets to hold the thread. Metallic threads tend to need room to unwind before running through the machine. For best results, allow distance between the spool and the threading area of the machine. Try operating the embroidery machine at a slower speed and with a looser tension to ensure successful results.

> *Lindee says: "Soft, cut-away backings are easier on metallic threads than stiff tear-away backings."*

It is sometimes recommended that metallic thread should pass through a thin layer of silicone to smooth the rough edges before it penetrates the fabric. Consult your sewing machine dealer first before adding any silicone to the thread since it may interfere with the mechanics of the machine.

Acrylic and Wool

Acrylic thread is similar to polyester thread in that it is colorfast. Its medium sheen provides a beautiful low luster effect when stitched. Acrylic thread is perfect for children's wear, is break resistant, and available in solid and variegated thread colors.

Wool thread is usually combined with another fiber, such as acrylic, to achieve the look of hand crewel embroidery. This thread is known for its fuzzy, matte appearance. For best results, use a larger needle (100 or 110) and a very low tension to accommodate for this thicker thread.

> *Lindee says: "Using specialty threads that are thicker than 40-weight rayon can produce problems with embroidery designs. Try enlarging designs without adding stitches to create more breathing room for the decorative threads."*

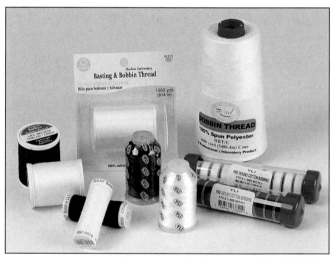

An assortment of bobbin thread from Coats & Clark, YLI, OESD, and Sulky.

Bobbin

A bobbin thread is designed to hold the decorative thread on the fabric. Unlike sewing where the same thread is used in the bobbin and the needle, in machine embroidery, bobbin threads are not the same as the decorative thread. It is best to use a thread specifically manufactured for use as a bobbin thread in high speed embroidery machines. Bobbin thread is available in several fiber contents and weights. It is best to use a thread specifically made for use as a bobbin-only thread. Bobbin thread should be strong and thin. Each type of bobbin thread has its own characteristics—from cotton to polyester, the difference is in the texture and strength of the

An assortment of acrylic and wool thread from YLI and Aero-fil.

thread. Some bobbin threads run more smoothly through the machine and will make the difference in the design. Cotton thread is softer next to the skin, where filament polyester is more coarse.

Bobbin thread comes standard in two colors—black and white. However, there are some cotton threads available in color coordinating 60-weight. This weight can be used in the bobbin to match with a decorative needle thread for reversible applications, such as bath towels or blankets.

There are several types of pre-wound bobbins available for use in commercial embroidery machines—bobbins with cardboard sides, plastic sides, or without sides. Pre-wound bobbins tend to jump during the embroidery process and can interfere with automatic thread cutters, so, it is best to check with your embroidery machine dealer to verify whether your machine will accept pre-wound bobbins.

For best results, wind your own blank bobbins that come with your machine. Purchase extra bobbins and wind several at a time to save time during the embroidery process.

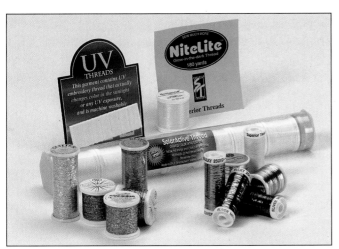

An assortment of specialty thread from SolarActive, YLI, Superior, and Sulky.

Specialty

There are several brands of specialty thread that are available to add sparkle, glitter, shine, or reflective pizzazz to any design. Note that some specialty threads work best when stitched alone in a design or from a vertical spool holder on the machine.

UV Activated Thread

This type of thread has the ability to change colors when exposed to sunlight. It's one color indoors and changes to a different color outdoors. The thread will return to its original color shortly after being removed from the sunlight.

Glow-in-the-Dark Thread

This type of thread is perfect for embroidering on garments used in the dark—such as kid's pajamas, Halloween costumes, night biking and running attire. The threads glow-in-the-dark after being activated by a light source for 30 minutes. There are some that sparkle by day and provide a sparkle glow-in-the-dark effect at night.

Threads that Sparkle

There are several brands and types of specialty thread that resemble vibrant glitter and shiny metal strips. The threads on the spool are vibrant and beautiful and look just radiant in decorative designs. For best results, use these specialty threads in open, airy designs or alone on fabric to show off their elegant characteristics. Treat these threads as you would a metallic thread. For best results, these specialty threads should be unwound off a vertical spool holder on the machine.

Small to large threads on spools and cones.

Spool/Cone Sizes

Threads come on holders in various sizes and yardages. From small spools to large cones, each size has its benefits. The smaller spools are great to start your thread collection. However, the smaller spools are wound tighter and have a tendency to kink when unwinding off the spool. Larger spools tend to unwind and run smoothly through the embroidery machine. In addition, basic colors on larger cones will last longer in your collection. Some larger spools will fit directly on your machine. Others are best suited for use on an independent thread stand next to,

31

or behind, the machine. The amount you embroider will determine the size spools to purchase. Bobbin thread is more economical when purchased on larger spools.

> *Patti Lee, consumer relations director for Sulky of America Inc., says: "Industry experts calculate that the average length of each stitch in embroidery designs to be around 4 to 5 mm. Based on this average, 22 yards of 40-weight rayon equals about 4,000 stitches. Therefore, a 250-yard spool can create 44,000 stitches, while an 850-yard spool can create 156,000 stitches."*

Thread Storage

Keep threads humidified; threads that dry out become brittle and will break often during the embroidery process. Therefore, store thread in drawers away from light and dust to keep them flexible. If you prefer to store threads on multiple spool stands, cover them with a dark cloth when not in use to protect from dust and light. Some thread spools have snap-lock ends to keep loose threads tidy. If not, use a self-stick tape to hold loose threads during storage.

Thread assortments from Brother, Coats & Clark, and Hoop-It-All.

Color Choices

Choosing thread colors for designs is similar to painting by number. The design digitizing companies dictate the number of colors in a design. Some companies provide thread color numbers for a particular brand. These color numbers are intended as guidelines only—you do not have to use the exact same color numbers. Be creative and let your imagination be your guide. If the design calls for three colors of red, choose three colors of red thread from your thread collection. Experiment with different colors

of threads for the ultimate creative experience. Thread colors are ultimately your creative decision.

> *Lindee recommends: "To make a design stand out, use two threads through a machine embroidery needle."*

Most threads come in a vast array of colors, with rayon and polyester providing the largest color selection. Some manufacturers sell basic thread color assortments in special packaging that may be cost saving and a great way to start a thread collection. When purchasing multiple spools of thread in one color, look for the color dye lot numbers and make sure they are the same. You may experience slight color changes in the dye lots from purchase to purchase of the same color number.

Threads that have multiple colors throughout the spool are called variegated threads. The colors change periodically throughout the spool in order to give a design multiple colors without changing threads. Variegated threads are not available in polyester fibers.

Two thin threads wound together to produce one spool of thread are considered a twisted multicolor thread. This thread creates the appearance of texture in decorative designs and is perfect for the petals of flowers or the fur on a teddy bear.

> *Annette Bailey, editor of* Creative Machine Embroidery *magazine, says: "Be adventurous when choosing your thread colors. Don't be governed by the thread numbers that accompany digitized designs. For example, if the next color in a design is Crimson Red #203, use any complementary red in your thread collection."*

Thread Color Charts

Most thread manufacturers sell charts of their stock colors, which are designed to provide accuracy when choosing colors for designs. Some charts are made from actual thread samples and provide the color number of the thread. Be sure to update your thread charts as new colors become available.

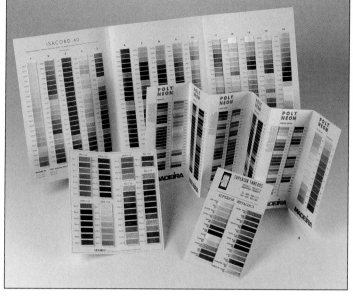

Exact match thread color charts from Madeira, OESD (Yenmet), and Superior.

Your Accessory Choices

Accessories for your embroidery equipment are timesavers and sometimes a necessity to assist you with the embroidery process. Here's a sampling of some products that you may find useful:

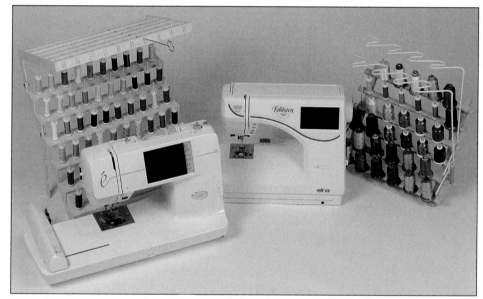

Thread Stands

Thread stands are designed to hold spools of thread during the embroidery process. Choose the thread colors for a design and place the spools on a thread stand. The stands will hold the threads vertically and can hold several spools of thread at a time.

Use the different levels of the thread stands to hold the colors of threads for several projects at a time. When the threads are not being used, cover the stand with a dark cloth to protect the threads from dust and light.

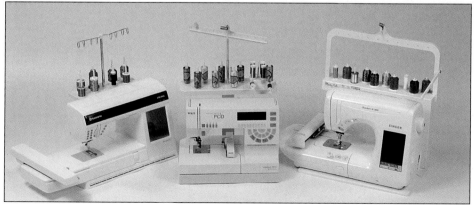

Thread stands from PD Sixty, June Tailor, Viking, and Cactus Punch (Martha Pullen).

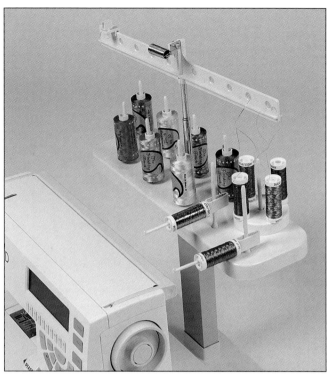

The Thread Palette® and The Horizontal Spool Holder from Mountainland Manufacturing.

Spool Holders

Vertical and horizontal spool holders are great for taming wild threads as they unwind off the spool. Attach the device onto the machine to hold a spool of thread at an angle which can help the spool unwind naturally off the holder.

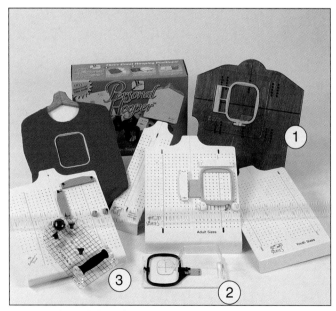

Hooping boards from The Perfect Hooper®, Sew Special and ABC Embroidery; the ClothSetter® from Janome and Elna, the Snappy from ABC Embroidery.

Garment Hooping Aids

Hooping boards are made especially for alignment of designs on garments. Designed with holes on the board for universal brackets that fit the shape of embroidery hoops, the hooping boards will provide you with a stable surface to help hoop your garment with ease. They are available in several styles for shirts, pants, and even children's clothes. Some boards are available with custom made, machine-specific hoop holders. (1)

A hoop cloth-setting device is available to take the guesswork out of alignment. Simply line up your template with the alignment arm inside the hoop and you'll have a perfectly set design every time. (2)

A hand-held, hoop setter will assist you in the hooping process by pushing the inner hoop into the outer hoop. Sewers who suffer from arthritis or carpal tunnel may find this device a necessity to ensure that the fabric is hooped taut. (3)

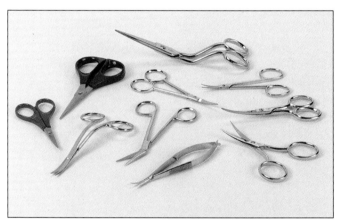

An assortment of scissors from Gingher, Elna, Baby Lock, Brother, and Tacony, Viking, Hummingbird House.

Scissors

The trimming of threads throughout the embroidery process is crucial. A sharp pair of close-cutting scissors is essential to have next to your machine at all times. Curved-tip scissors of all sizes and styles are your best choice. The curved tip will aid in clipping threads close to the stitching. Standard sewing scissors are also required for cutting stabilizers. Cutaway stabilizers tend to dull the blades of scissors quickly, therefore, consider purchasing several pair.

Surge Protector

It is advisable to guard embroidery equipment against electrical current surges and lightning strikes. Purchase a high quality surge protector with more than four outlets and a telephone jack for an Internet connection. By purchasing a quality surge protector, you are protecting the thousands of dollars invested in your embroidery equipment.

Vicki Madigan, education consultant for Brother International, says: "When purchasing computerized sewing and embroidery equipment be sure to purchase a quality serge protector. Treat this equipment as you would your television or home computer."

Other necessities for embroidery, from transparency film to thread nets.

Other Products

Soldering Iron

A soldering iron is used to melt and seal the cut fabric edges of a dimensional embroidery motif to prevent the unraveling of the base fabric or stitching. For best results, use a nylon base fabric and a 15-watt soldering iron. Use this tool with a light, swift touch on the outside edges of a motif to prevent burning the fabric and stitches. Look for a soldering iron that has a pointed tip and the option to replace the tips. A wood burning tool, stencil burner, or hot knife can also be used.

Linda McGehee, owner of Ghee's and the industry expert on dimensional embroidery, says: "Keep the tips of your tool clean by using a specialty soldering iron cleaner. The nylon can blacken the tip during the fabric melting process. This black melted substance can transfer to light-colored fabrics if the tips aren't properly cleaned. Replace tips as needed."

(See Dimensional Embroidery and Fringing for more tips from Linda.)

Tack Iron

This product is used with an ironing board and is just small enough to fit inside the hoop to fuse decorative appliqué material onto the hooped base fabric.

Stitch Remover

Similar in appearance to a hair-trimming device, a stitch remover is used on the wrong side of a project to remove the bobbin threads that hold the design in place. It has been designed specially for stitch removal and will remove a majority of embroidery stitches.

Temporary Marking Pen/Pencil

A temporary marking pen or pencil, such as a water-soluble marking pen, is essential to have on hand for marking fabric. After the stitching process, simply touch water to the mark and it disappears. It is important to know that the heat of an iron will render the mark of a water-soluble pen permanent. Be sure to remove all marks before ironing the fabric. A chalk pencil is another form of temporary marking device.

Transparency Film

Transparency film is a clear sheet of plastic that is available in write-on, printer or copy machine sheets. It is used for template making which will aid in the alignment of designs.

Thread Nets and Holders

Thread nets look like hairnets and prevent the thread from unwinding faster than the machine can uptake the thread during the embroidery process. They are also perfect for holding loose threads on the spool while being stored.

A self-stick tape can be wrapped around a spool of thread to prevent it from unraveling off the spool. It comes in a roll just like packing tape and it holds hard-to-store threads.

Lindee says: "I like to use a fiber dissolving fluid for my specialty techniques, such as cutwork and edgework. A very, very fine line of this fluid is used next to the stitching to dissolve the fabric. For best results, use on natural fabric with synthetic thread."

Chapter 3

The Embroidery Process

Your Fabric Choices
An Overview and Reference Guide

he garments or fabrics chosen for embroidery are critical for the success of a project. Not every design will work on every fabric. The same design may vary in the way it stitches on different types of fabrics. Designs are digitized for an average fabric—polyester/cotton woven fabric such as poplin. Any variation from this average fabric will result in changes to every part of the embroidery process—threads, stabilizers, fabric, hoop, tension, etc. It is important for you to determine the types of designs that are best to use on the fabrics you choose. For example, a dense, high stitch count design is not appropriate for knit fabrics, but would be more appropriate for a stable woven fabric. An open and airy mini design is not appropriate for Polarfleece fabrics, but would be more appropriate for knits.

Designs are best stitched on a solid color material, which will make the best backdrop for embroidery. Keep in mind that an embroidery design on a garment carries an image and is usually one of the first things to catch the eye of others.

The following information will provide you with suggested products to use on certain fabrics for the embroidery process. For best results, test-stitch designs onto fabric the same or similar to the fabric used in the project. (See test-stitching on page 48.)

Sample of design on sweatshirt fabric; embroidery by Dakota Collectibles®.

Knits
(interlock fabric, sweatshirts, T-shirts)

Knits are considered an unstable fabric since they tend to stretch during the hooping and embroidery process. It is recommended to eliminate the stretch of knits before the hooping process by fusing a tricot interfacing to the backside of the fabric perpendicular to the stretch of the fabric. Or use an iron-on or a cut-away stabilizer secured to the back of the fabric. It is not advisable to use tear-away stabilizers on knit fabrics since the needle penetrations tend to break down the tear-away stabilizer and distort the fabric. It is advisable to use a water-soluble topping to hold the stitches on top of the fabric.

Interfacing:	Fusible tricot knit perpendicular to the stretch of the fabric
Stabilizer:	Cut-away iron-on or adhesive
Topping:	Water-soluble
Needle:	Ballpoint
Thread:	Polyester, acrylic, cotton
Design:	A large, low stitch count design or a design with long stitches

Sample of design on denim; embroidery by Dakota Collectibles

Denim/Twill (light and heavy)

Denim and twill are considered unstable fabrics because of their cross-grain stretch. Even though they are a woven fabric, treat them as a knit. If the denim is heavy, use cut-away stabilizer and the hoopless embroidery method found on page 47. If the denim is light, use a spray adhesive to adhere the

36

stabilizer to the denim before hooping or use a cut-away iron-on stabilizer. Be sure to use a larger needle on heavier denim.

Interfacing:	Fusible tricot knit (optional)
Stabilizer:	Cut-away
Topping:	Water-soluble (optional)
Needle:	Sharp
Thread:	Cotton, polyester, acrylic
Design:	All types

Lindee's tip: "Stitching very dense designs on heavier-weight denim can cause "cupping". If the fabric threads are closely packed together, then there is little breathing room to stitch the design. The embroidery threads will push the fabric fibers apart, which can result in cupping after the design is stitched. Use a heavy cut-away stabilizer to hold your fabric and enlarge your design slightly to offer more breathing room for the thread."

Sample of embroidery on quilter's cotton; Elna design.

Tightly-woven Fabrics

Tightly-woven fabrics vary in weight and density as well as in fiber content. Some of the most common fabrics in this category are cotton, broadcloth, and canvas. They are the most stable fabrics and produce good results with any embroidery application.

Interfacing:	None
Stabilizer:	Tear-away or cut-away
Topping:	Not necessary
Needle:	Sharp or Embroidery
Thread:	Any
Design:	Any

Loosely-woven Fabrics

Loosely-woven fabrics vary in weight and density as well as in fiber content. Some of the most common fabrics in this category are linen, crepe, and some wool. Be aware that some of these fabrics tend to shift during the hooping process. Spray starch an open weave fabric, such as linen, before the stabilizing process to keep it from shifting.

Sample of design on linen; embroidery by Dakota Collectibles.

Interfacing:	Optional
Stabilizer:	Cut-away—mesh for light-colored fabric
Topping:	None
Needle:	Sharp or embroidery
Thread:	Rayon, polyester, cotton, acrylic
Design:	Open and airy low stitch count designs or designs with long stitches

Polarfleece (high-pile fabrics)

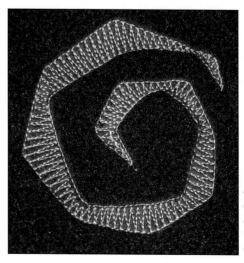

Sample of design on Polarfleece; Cactus Punch design.

Polarfleece, velvet and velour fabrics have a high pile that should be treated differently than any other type of fabric. These fabrics should not be hooped since they are prone to hoop-burn—the crushing of the pile from being crushed between the inner and outer hoops. Therefore, these fabrics are best used with the hoopless embroidery method (see page 47). High-pile fabrics are best embroidered with a topping to prevent the threads from becoming imbedded into the fabric. Most pile fabrics do not tolerate the touch of an iron. Therefore, an iron-on stabilizer may not be appropriate since it could compress the pile during the ironing process. When using a topping, be sure to check the washability of the fabric before using a water-soluble topping. It may be necessary to use a permanent vinyl topping instead. Choose designs that have quality underlay stitches to compress the fibers before stitching the design. Sometimes just stitching the underlay of a design can make a nice effect on Polarfleece fabrics.

Interfacing:	None
Stabilizer:	Cut-away
Topping:	Water-soluble or vinyl cover-up
Needle:	Ballpoint
Thread:	Polyester, Acrylic (Rayon for Velvet)
Design:	Open satin-stitched designs, Polarfleece texturizing designs and large low stitch count designs

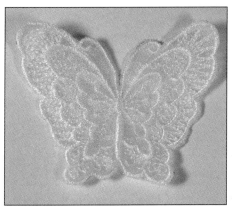

Sample of embroidery on sparkle organza; Brother design.

Sheer and Specialty Fabrics

With just a little extra care, successful embroidery on sheer or specialty fabrics is possible. Sheer fabric tends to shift during the hooping process. Consider hooping the stabilizer and use a temporary spray adhesive to secure the fabric to the stabilizer. For hard to embroider specialty bridal fabrics, consider stitching designs onto netting or nylon organdy/organza and then stitching the motif onto the specialty fabric. (See Dimensional Embroidery on page 61.) Sheer fabrics can be hooped with another piece of sheer fabric as the stabilizer. Place the stabilizer piece of sheer fabric perpendicular to the base sheer fabric for added stability.

Interfacing:	None
Stabilizer:	None, lightweight tear-away, poly-mesh or water-soluble (if appropriate for the fabric) or organza sheer fabric
Topping:	None or water soluble (if appropriate for the fabric)
Needle:	Fine sharp
Thread:	Lightweight
Design:	Open, airy, light designs

Pauline Richards is the editor of the Total Embellishment Newsletter, *and a freelance writer for both* Sew News *and* Creative Machine Embroidery. *Pauline says: "I like working with a very thick water-soluble stabilizer when stitching on sheers. I also prefer to use a lightweight embroidery thread color coordinating in the bobbin as well as the needle. Since the upper thread and the bobbin thread match, I don't have to worry about the bobbin thread showing from the right side. Although I have to change the bobbin each time I change the upper thread color, the end result is well worth the effort. I use this technique for any reversible embroidery application."*

Sample of embroidery on toweling with and without a water-soluble topping; embroidery by Pellon.

Toweling

Embroidery on terry cloth toweling makes personalization fun. This fabric requires a topping to compress the looped fibers while stitching embroidery designs. Do not limit yourself to just monogram designs—add some creativity with decorative designs, too. This heavy-weight fabric is best when used with the hoopless embroidery method found on page 47.

Interfacing:	None
Stabilizer:	Adhesive
Topping:	Water-soluble or cover-up (plain or adhesive)
Needle:	Universal
Thread:	Polyester, acrylic
Design:	All designs especially monogram letters

> *Lindee says: "I often omit backings when appliquéing on towels. Most appliqués are 'low-impact' meaning they won't distort the fabric and towels and are fairly stable. This eliminates having to pick out exposed backing within the appliqué making a softer and more attractive back to the design."*

Fabric Nap

Some fabrics have a nap—a directional texture to the pile on the right side of the fabric. Polarfleece®, velvet and velour are examples of fabrics with a nap. It is important that you take into consideration the nap of the fabric when stitching decorative designs. In most cases, a topping will be necessary on these fabrics to hold down the pile of the fabric during the stitching process. If you experience the fibers of the fabric poking up through the stitches after the embroidery process, try a vinyl cover-up topping in place of the water-soluble topping. The vinyl is permanent and will hold down the fibers under the stitching. It will tear away from the design after the embroidery process. Be sure to test-stitch designs since some designs are not suited for fabrics with a nap.

Difficult Fabrics

Uneven surfaces of fabric can deflect the needle during the embroidery process and cause a lot of embroidery problems. The edges of the embroidery will not be smooth and the thread will look jagged. Keep in mind that there are some fabrics that are not suited for embroidery. It may be necessary to change the project fabric to one that is suited for embroidery.

> *Lindee recommends: "For fabrics with a heavy, coarse weave such as duck cloth, or canvas, a topping will not solve the problem. These heavy fabrics will deflect the needle causing a jagged, stair-step look as the stitches are placed first on one side and then the other of the fabric's weave. This is what we call an embroidery fact of life!"*

Fabric Care

For machine washable fabrics, it is best to preshrink your fabric or item to be embroidered before starting the stitching process. By pre-washing your fabric, you'll be rinsing any starch, sizing, or bleach from the fabric. In addition, pre-washing the fabric will help eliminate distortion of designs after the embroidery process. If your garment or fabric is dry-clean only, be sure to use thread and stabilizers that are compatible with the dry cleaning process.

Purchased Embroidery Items

If you own a garment that has been embroidered in a factory, there is a possibility the garment was not pre-washed or pre-shrunk before the embroidery process. Therefore, special laundry care will be necessary to prevent the warping of the embroidery. Before washing the item for the first time, turn the garment to the wrong side and press the design with an iron on a padded ironing board. This step will set the design to the fabric. Wash the garment in cold water on the gentle cycle and tumble dry on a low heat for a few moments to remove the wrinkles. Hang the garment to finish drying. Press the design again, on the wrong side, after it has dried to smooth out any cupping, ridges or rough edges.

Off-the-rack Items (blanks)

If you purchase garments at a clothing store to embroider, be sure to pre-wash the garment. It is also possible to purchase items called "blanks". This is the term the commercial embroidery industry uses for garments or items that are made of solid colored fabric for embroidery. Look for companies that sell blank garments for embroidery (see Resources on page 136).

Design Placement

One of the first steps in the embroidery process is to determine where you want to stitch your design. Designs can be randomly placed or precisely positioned on a project. The decision is a challenge in creativity. You have the freedom to be as imaginative with the placement as you are with the selection and colors of a design. The following measurements are suggested guidelines for the placement of designs. As with all aspects of embroidery, allow your personal preference to be your guide.

Note: All placements are for the center of the design area unless otherwise noted.

*Bath Linens**   *Bed Linens**

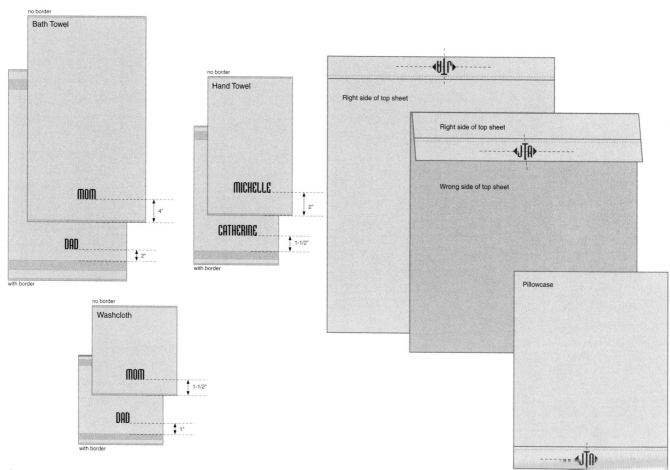

*Note: Stitch the motif at the opposite end of the manufacturer's tag/label

Washcloth—1-1/2" above the hem or 1" above the border; for washcloths with no border, use a diagonal corner placement
Hand towel—2" above the hem or 1-1/2" above the border
Bath towel—4" above the hem or 2" above the border

Top sheet—Center the lower edge 2" above the header or centered on the header (upside down on the right side of the sheet)
Pillowcase—Center on the header

Garments

Hats

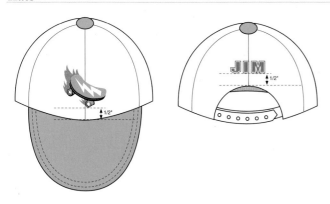

Hats—front motif centered 1/2" above where the bill meets the cap; back motif centered 1/2" above the half circle opening.

Shirt Cuffs

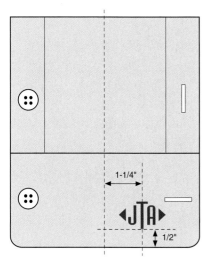

Shirt cuffs—on the left cuff only; 1-1/4" from the center toward the buttonhole and 1/2" from the bottom edge.

Shirt Pockets

Shirt pockets—centered between the hem and top edge in the center of the pocket.

Shirt Yokes

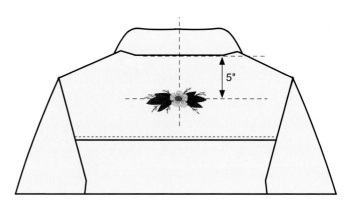

Yoke of shirts—centered and 1" above the yoke seam.

Shirt Pockets

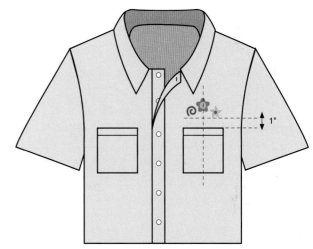

Above shirt pockets—bottom of the design 1" from the pocket edge.

Bowling Shirts

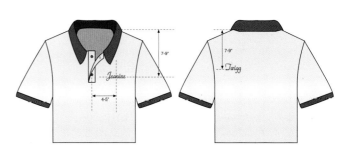

Bowling shirts—first name on the front 7" to 9" down from the left shoulder and 4-5" from the center; last name on the back right with the same measurements.

Socks

Socks—1/2" from the fold line by the anklebone.

Turtlenecks

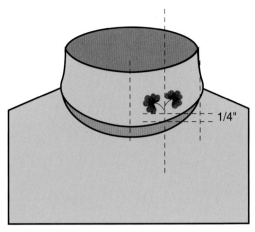

Turtlenecks—1-1/2" from the center and leave 1/2" from the top of the design to the turtleneck fold.

Polo Shirts

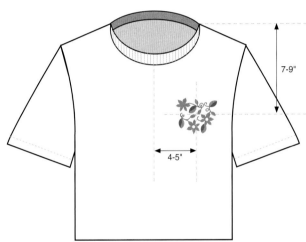

Polo shirt/T-shirts—7" to 9" down from the left shoulder seam and 4-5" from the center.

Sweatshirts

Sweatshirts—centered 3" to 4"down from the neck edge of the fabric.

Shorts

Shorts—on the shorts front, 1" between the side of the design and the side seam; 1/2" between the bottom of the design and top of the hem.

Blankets

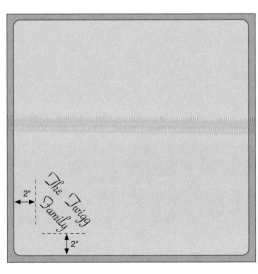

Blankets—diagonally placed in the corner of the blanket 2" from the side edges.

Monogramming

Photo provided by Embroideryarts.

Monogramming is the embroidery technique that uses one or more letters as the initials of a name and is commonly used on towels, bed linens, and clothing for identification or decorative purposes.

Here are some hints and tips provided by Richards Jarden from Embroideryarts, a division of Intarsia Arts.

For proper placement of initials within the monogram Richards suggests:

"The most conventional monogram arrangement consists of three letters—a larger central letter, flanked by two smaller letters, one on each side. One and two letter monograms also are traditional. It is typical that the center letter is the surname or last name, with the letter on the left representing the first name or birth name, and the letter on the right representing the middle name."

"A married couple might choose to blend their individual initials into a common traditional monogram—for example, John R. Smith, who marries Katherine L. Jones, might create the common monogram JSK."

"There is some flexibility in the placement of monograms on projects. Be as creative with your placement as you are with your design and thread choices to make each monogram original and interesting. Use Jeanine's placement guidelines found on page 40 to locate the suggested placement of a monogram. Embroideryarts recommends stitching a sample of the monogram and making a paper template from a photocopy of the design. Then, cut away the excess paper surrounding the monogram. Locate the center of the monogram by measuring the height and width, and then mark lines that intersect between each dimension. Use a standard hole-punch to punch a hole at the center point. Use this paper template to locate the center of the design on the fabric. Mark the placement with a water-soluble marker and stitch the monogram."

Design Alignment

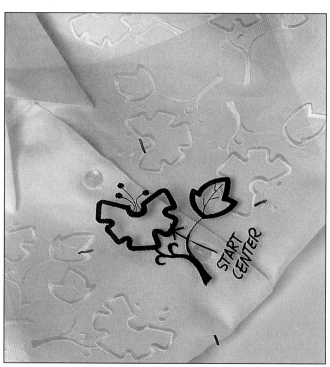

Transparency film template; Cactus Punch design.

The alignment of a design on a project is one of the most important steps in the embroidery process. It can make the difference between an off-centered project and one that has been perfectly stitched in a narrow area.

Marking the Fabric

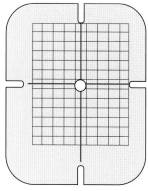

Most embroidery machine hoops come packaged with a template the size of the inner hoop. The template fits snuggly inside the hoop. It has cutouts that match up with the notches on the hoop and a hole for the center/starting point of designs. Keep in mind that the center of the hoop may not be the center of the design. Be sure to double-check the hoop markings to determine the center of the design. Use the measurements found on pages 40-42 to locate the suggested placement of the design or be creative and choose a random position.

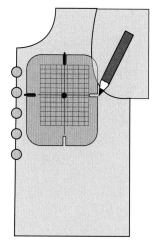

1. Once you've located the placement of the design, use a temporary marking pen/pencil to place a dot representing the center/starting point of the design.

2. Use the appropriate hoop template to align the mark on the fabric with the hole near the center of the template. On the garment, mark the placement of the four notch grooves and remove the template from the fabric.

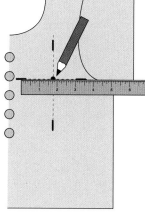

3. Using a ruler, connect the notch marks vertically and horizontally on the fabric.

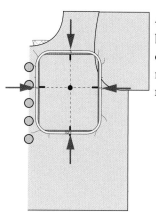

4. When hooping the fabric, be sure to align the marks on the fabric with the hoop markings for precise placement.

Note: If an iron-on stabilizer or interfacing will be used, be sure to fuse the material to the fabric before the marking process since water-soluble markers become permanent with the heat of an iron.

44

Design Templates

Design templates from Janome, Elna, Viking, Baby Lock, and computer generated.

Some manufacturers of digitized designs provide life-sized templates of designs. These templates provide the exact size of the design to aid you with the placement process. Use these templates in combination with your hoop template to determine the exact placement of the design. Here are the types of templates you'll find useful for design alignment:

Paper

Some companies offer a life-size template of designs printed on paper and are provided with the design disk pack. Use a transparency marker to trace the design onto the hoop template. Be sure to test and use a transparency marker that will wipe away with water for the next project. Scan or make copies onto transparency film, too.

Clear Plastic

Some companies provide a life-size template of the design on clear plastic that is provided with designs. Align the clear plastic template over the hoop template to aid in the alignment of the design onto the project.

Computer Generated

You can also generate templates from your computer. Transfer or load designs into a customizing or editing software that is compatible with your embroidery machine. Print a copy of the design onto paper or transparency film appropriate for your printer. Be sure the software can print the design in its true size. Another type of computer template can be made with a scanner. Scan a test-stitch sample into a computer and print a copy onto paper or transparency film.

Example of transparency film template.

Transparency Film

The most precise alignment aid is a template made from transparency film. Print or photo copy a test-stitch sample using a transparency film that is specially made for an ink-jet printer, laser printer or copy machine. For best results, test-stitch the sample with dark colored thread.

After the design has been printed onto the transparency film, trace the hoop template and markings onto the film. Cut the film to the exact size of the hoop template for ease in design placement. Make transparency film templates from paper templates, too.

How to Hoop

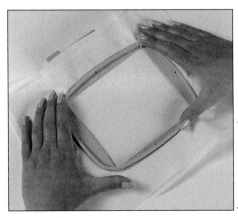

Proper placement of hands while standing to hoop the stabilizer with the fabric.

To hoop or not to hoop, that is the question! The term "hoop" has two definitions. The word hoop, used as a noun, is the two-piece device that holds the fabric and stabilizer during the embroidery process. The word hoop, used as a verb, is the action of holding the fabric and stabilizer taut during the embroidery process; usually referred to as the process of hooping.

Proper hooping techniques are important to the end result of a project. By hooping a project correctly, you can prevent a design from becoming distorted, warped or out of alignment during the embroidery process.

45

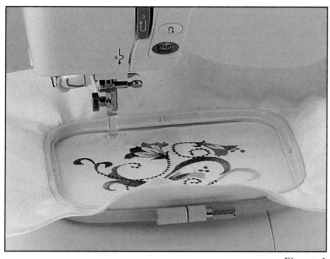

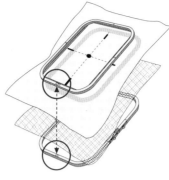

3. Lay the inner hoop over the fabric; make sure the inner hoop's main directional arrow mark is facing the same direction as the outer hoop. These arrows must always be in alignment to ensure the design will be centered in the hoop.

Figure 1

Hoop Tension

The screw attached to the outer hoop holds the tension between the fabric and the stabilizer (see Figure 1). It is important to set the tension before hooping your fabric.

Therefore, test-hoop your fabric with the stabilizer several times to get the proper hoop tension. Loosen or tighten the screw on the outer hoop to achieve the perfect tension. Once the tension is set, start the hooping process. It is not advisable to loosen or tighten the screw once the fabric is in the hoop. This can cause hoop burn and other tension-related difficulties.

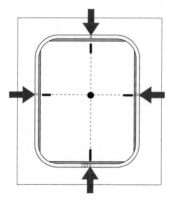

4. Align the fabric markings along with the notches on the outer hoop. Shift the fabric until the outer and inner hoops are aligned with the marks on the fabric.

The Hooping Process—Step-by-step

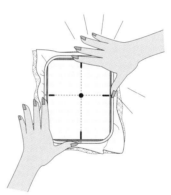

5. Begin the hooping process at the furthest point away from the screw on the outer hoop. With both hands, press the hoop into place by walking your fingers over the outer hoop toward the end with the screw until the inner hoop snaps into place.

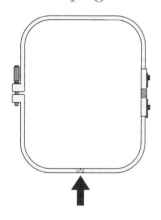

1. Place the outer hoop on a firm, flat surface.

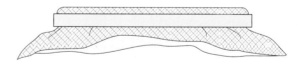

6. Push the inner hoop slightly deeper than the outer hoop. There should be a slight ridge protruding past the outer hoop and the fabric should ride on the bed of the machine during the embroidery process.

2. Place the marked fabric with the stabilizer over the hoop. If necessary, use a spray adhesive to secure the two layers together. Be sure to spray only the stabilizer.

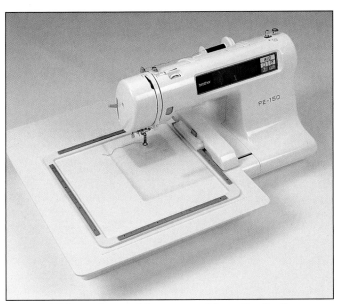

Hoop-It-All frame hoop with support table on the Brother home "embroidery only" machine.

Hoopless Embroidery

The easiest way of hooping fabric is to use the hoopless embroidery method. This method uses adhesive stabilizer secured to the backside of the hoop or a frame to securely hold the fabric during the embroidery process. This press-on method is perfect for fabrics that should not be hooped, such as Polarfleece®, velvet and velour. Hard to hoop bulky fabrics, such as toweling, can also benefit from this method.

Using a Standard Hoop

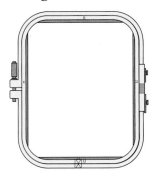

1. Place both the inner and outer hoops together and completely tighten the tension screw.

2. Cut a piece of adhesive stabilizer slightly larger than the hoop. Peel back the paper and lay the stabilizer on a flat surface with the adhesive side facing up.

3. Place the hoop directly over the adhesive stabilizer and press into place.

4. Place the item to be embroidered onto the adhesive backed stabilizer. Finger press the item in place within the hoop—pins can also be used for added security.

Alternative method: Hoop a piece of the adhesive-backed stabilizer. Use a pin to score the paper on the inside of the hoop and peel away the paper. Place the item to be embroidered onto the adhesive-backed stabilizer.

Using a Frame Hoop

Another product that can be used with your machine for hoopless embroidery is a frame hoop. This type of hoop does not have an inner ring, but rather an outer flange that holds the adhesive stabilizer in place. They are available in several sizes to fit specific machine brands. Large frame hoops may require a separate stand to keep the hoop level during the embroidery process. Use a frame hoop as you would the two machine hoops together. Secure the stabilizer to the backside of the frame and secure the fabric to the stabilizer.

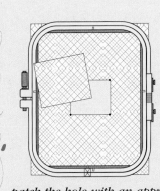

Lindee says: "I use adhesive backings as a hooping aid, not a stabilizer. Since these backings can make your embroidery feel thick and stiff, I often cut a hole in the backing slightly larger than my design and then patch the hole with an appropriate stabilizer for the fabric. I stitch my design through the hole in the adhesive backing and allow the remainder of the adhesive surface to hold my garment in place during the embroidery process. This is the only time I might use a hoop larger than necessary for my design in order to give me more adhesive area to grip my fabric."

Making Your Own Adhesive Stabilizer

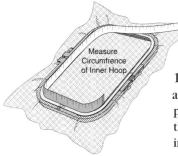

1. To make your own adhesive stabilizer, hoop a piece of stabilizer. Measure the circumference of the inner hoop as illustrated.

2. Cut a piece of cardboard 6" tall by the circumference of the hoop. Tape the short 6" ends together.

3. Insert the cardboard piece into the hoop and lightly spray the stabilizer with adhesive inside the cardboard. The cardboard prevents the hoop from becoming sticky with the spray adhesive.

Basting

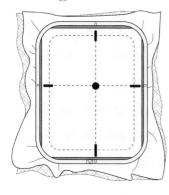

Once the fabric and stabilizer are secured to the hoop or frame, it may be necessary to baste the layers together with long sewing machine stitches around the perimeter of the hoop. This process will secure the stabilizer to the fabric. Some embroidery machines have the capability of auto-basting around the design area. Check the owner's manual for this capability.

Hooping with an Alignment Board

There are several types of hoop alignment boards that make wonderful hooping aids. They work with your standard machine hoops (with board adapters) to help hoop projects with ease.

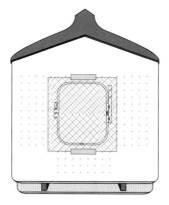

1. Simply mark the location of the design on the garment. Place the hoop on the board in the exact location to align the design. Tape a piece of the appropriate stabilizer over the hoop.

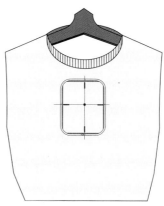

2. Slip the garment over the board and using the inner hoop as your guide, hoop the garment using the board for support. Remove the entire hoop with the garment from the board and it will be ready for stitching.

Hooping boards are also used for embroidery production when multiple garments are being hooped in the same location.

Ready, Set, Embroider!

Now it's time to put it all together and start the embroidery process. The first step is the practice test-stitching process of pre-stitching a design to verify that it is compatible with the fabric, stabilizer, threads, and method before embroidering on the real project. Once you are satisfied with the end result of your test-stitch sample, you can stitch on the real project with confidence. (See Appendix 2 for a test-stitching form that will assist with this process.)

Testing 1, 2, 3...

One of the most important steps of the embroidery process is to test-stitch a design on a piece of fabric the same or similar to the fabric of a project. This step will save you time and heartache should the design not be stitched correctly. Please do not ignore this step—it is not a waste of time and thread. It will actually save you from making mistakes on the real project, which could be far more costly. In addition, the test-stitch process will provide you with the means to create an alignment template for the project. (See page 45 for instructions on making templates.)

> *Lindee's tip: "When testing, make sure you hoop your test fabric in the same orientation as the "real" project. Fabric hooped "willy-nilly" can react differently due to the grain of fabric."*

If you will be sewing your project from scratch, purchase a 1/4 yard of extra fabric for the test-stitch process. If you will be purchasing "blank" garments for embroidery, purchase 1/4 yard of fabric the same or similar to that of your project at a local fabric store. After purchasing the fabric, pre-wash the fabric.

How to Embroider Step-by-step

Follow the embroidery steps below to test-stitch a sample of the design on a piece of fabric the same or similar to your project fabric. For best results, use a piece of fabric and stabilizer substantially larger than your hoop. Be sure to trim threads between color changes. There may be times during the embroidery process that a design may jump from one location to another on the fabric. Be sure to stop the machine during the embroidery process to trim "jump-stitch" threads. It's important to trim away long threads that may get caught or inappropriately buried or caught underneath other stitches in the design.

1. Select a design suitable for the project.

2. Select an appropriate stabilizer for the project fabric. Cut a piece of stabilizer larger than the size of the hoop.

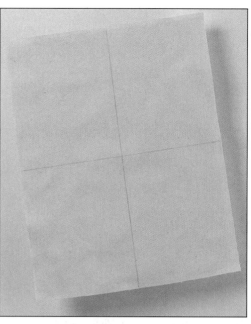

3. Mark the placement of the design on the fabric with a temporary marking pen or pencil.

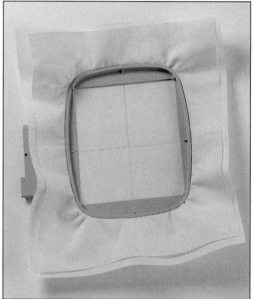

4. Hoop the fabric with the stabilizer. Be sure to align the fabric marking with the notches on the hoop.

5. Load the design onto the machine.

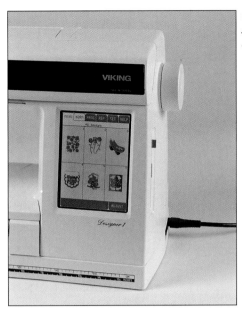

6. *Locate and select the design on the machine.*

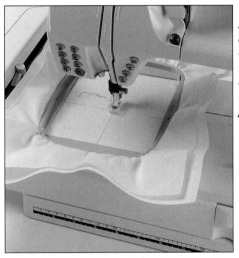

7. *Attach the hoop to the embroidery arm. Center the needle directly over the intersecting placement mark.*

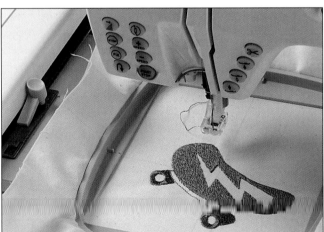

8. *Load the machine with the first color of thread. Start the embroidery process to stitch the first color of the design. When the machine stops, trim any exposed loose threads. Change to the next color thread and restart the machine. Continue until the design is complete. Remove the hoop from the arm of the machine. Trim any loose threads on top of the fabric and clip any bobbin threads within 1/2" from the fabric.*

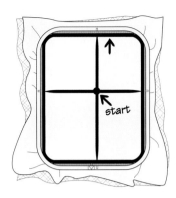

Before removing the test fabric from the hoop, mark the fabric with a thin permanent marker where the fabric and the inner hoop intersect. Mark the fabric with an arrow pointing upward to indicate the top of the design. Mark the center and/or starting points on the fabric. Re-mark the cross on the fabric; make sure both the horizontal and vertical lines meet at the center of the design. Marking the fabric in this manner will help design alignment and for making a template.

Check the Sample

Remove the fabric from the hoop and use these guidelines to determine if the sample was stitched properly and how to fix any problems:

Are the stitches raised and smooth?
Quick fix: Press on the wrong side or adjust the tension.

Does the underside of the satin stitches show too much or too little bobbin thread?
Quick fix: Adjust the tension.

Does the underside of the running stitches show too much or very little bobbin thread?
Quick fix: Adjust the tension.

Does the topside of the design show bobbin thread?
Quick fix: Adjust the tension.

Is there puckering around the outside of the design?
Quick fix: Change the stabilizer; hoop the fabric taut; change to a less dense design; change the tension.

Are there threads looping on the top of the design?
Quick fix: Change the needle, thread and/or adjust the tension.

Are there holes marks around the design?
Quick fix: Use a smaller needle and thread.

Does the design hold up after washing?
Quick fix: Change the stabilizer.

Did the outline stitch align perfectly around the design?
Quick fix: Change the stabilizer; check for hoop interference.

Are there gaps in the stitching?
Quick fix: Use thicker thread; change the stabilizer; reduce the design slightly.

Did the threads sink into the fabric?
Quick fix: Use a water-soluble topping or permanent vinyl; adjust the tension.

Did the design shift during the embroidery process?
Quick fix: Check for hoop interference; make sure the project is not too heavy for the hoop; machine may be overheating; design may be corrupted during the computer transfer process.

Do you like the colors?
Quick fix: Now is the best time to change thread colors.

Did the tear-away stabilizer fall off the project?
Quick fix: Use a cut-away stabilizer; change to a less dense design.

Does the design feel too stiff for the fabric?
Quick fix: Change to a less dense design; use a lighter thread and/or stabilizer.

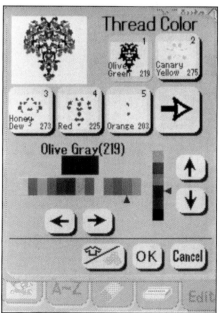

Changing thread colors on the screen of a Janome embroidery machine.

Does the design curl after washing?
Quick fix: Use a cut-away stabilizer; change to a less compact design.

Consult the troubleshooting section on page 125 for more tips.

Make necessary changes according to the results of the test-stitch. Continue the test-stitch process until you are satisfied with the finished results.

Machine Tension

Don't be afraid to change the tension on your machine. Most machines have auto tension settings, but there are many variables that can affect the stitching process. Therefore, play with the embroidery machine tension during the test-stitch process to achieve the look you need for your design. Note that adding more stabilizers to a design can cause tension problems. Therefore, adjust your tension accordingly.

Keep a Notebook of Test Stitches

After successfully completing the test-stitching process, save the sample(s) in a notebook. These samples will become an important part of your embroidery knowledge—refer to them when making future projects with the same or similar fabric. Make a photocopy of the Test Stitch Evaluation Form found on page 131. Write the necessary information onto the sheet pertaining to the test-stitch. Keep the Test Stitch Evaluation Sheet, your sample stitch-out, and a template of the design in a sheet protector inside a 3-ring notebook dedicated for your samples. Refer to these samples when stitching on similar fabrics in the future.

Finishing

The design is not complete until after the finishing process, which includes the trimming of threads and the pressing of the design. The trimming includes cutting the top loose threads close to the fabric. On the backside of the design, trim bobbin threads to within 1/2" from the fabric to avoid clipping the tie-off stitches. It is important to press the design after the embroidery process to set the design into the fabric. Always press on the wrong side of the fabric on a padded ironing board with a press cloth. Use the lowest steam iron setting to set the design.

Sara Meyer-Snuggerud, director of marketing for OESD, says: "Your embroidery is not finished until the last trimming is done. Always clip close to the stitching on the front. Now the back, that's a different story. If you have a jump stitch of bobbin on the back that is big enough to catch a finger in, cut it in half. If you can't catch a finger, the thread can and should remain intact. Do not cut close to the stitching. Always leave at least 1/2" or more of the bobbin thread hanging. This alleviates any threat of trimming those valuable lock stitches."

Get to Know Your Machine

It is important to get to know your machine and how it stitches. Don't be surprised to discover that your machine may not work with every thread, stabilizer, or embroidery product you try. It may be necessary for you to experiment stitching designs with a variety of threads and embroidery supplies. The tension, timing, and speed of your machine are unique, and these factors will dictate the products that your machine will tolerate.

NEVER LEAVE AN EMBROIDERY MACHINE UNATTENDED WHILE IT IS STITCHING.

Anything could happen during your absence—from the fabric getting caught under the needle to a needle or thread breaking. Any number of problems could arise that could yield disastrous results if the machine is left unattended.

Changing Designs

There will be times when a design is not the exact size, style, or color. Here are some of the ways you can manipulate designs by changing, scaling, or only using a portion of a design:

On-screen Design Changes

Editing changes can be made to designs on the touch-screen of an embroidery machine. From enlarging and reducing to combining designs, use the touch-screen of the machine to make the necessary changes to the design. Consult your owner's manual for on-screen design change instructions. If you are unable to manipulate the designs on your embroidery machine it may be necessary to transfer the designs to your computer to make any changes.

Using a Portion of a Design

Most designs can be stitched with different thread colors. At each change in color, the embroidery machine will stop for a change in thread color. You can also forward through a design by color to choose a particular part of the design to stitch. For example, you can forward through the colors to choose a simple leaf or a flower to stitch without having to stitch the entire design. Most design packs come with color change information. Consult this information to determine which part of the design can be stitched separately according to the color changes or test-stitch the entire design noting color changes and portions of the designs that can be stitched separately.

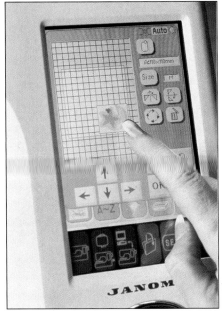

Touch screen of a Janome embroidery machine.

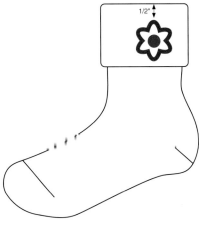

Use only the flower from the design on the CD included with book.

20% Larger

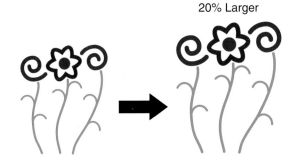

Scaling Designs

Scaling, sometimes referred to as "sizing", is the process of enlarging or reducing a design to fit your specifications. The scaling of a design can be accomplished on the screen of an embroidery machine or by using a brand specific software package. Consult your owner's manual on how to scale designs on your machine.

The company that digitized the design determines the stitch count. The stitch count refers to the number of stitches that makes up the design. The larger the number, the more stitches there are and the denser the design. It is important to maintain the integrity of the stitches when changing a design. If the stitch count remains the same as the design is enlarged, the design will stitch onto the fabric with spaces between the stitches. Make sure the embroidery machine or computer software can compensate for the design change and add more stitches. Consult your owner's manual for this feature.

If the design is too densely stitched for the fabric or if you want to use a thicker thread to stitch the design, enlarge the design slightly without changing the stitch count to open up the space between the stitches. Also, a thicker thread will compensate for the space between stitches without changing a design. Or, a thinner thread will allow the easier stitching of dense designs.

Combining Designs

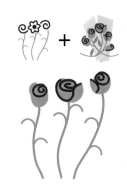

The possibilities are endless when combining designs. Some embroidery machines will allow the combining of designs directly on the embroidery machine. Or, combine and save designs on the computer and transfer the designs to the embroidery machine. Consult your equipment owner's manual on how to combine designs on your embroidery machine or computer software.

Making Your Own Designs

With the aid of the brand-specific software for your embroidery equipment, you'll have the ability to draw, scan and digitize designs. Try using clipart from other computer software packages to digitize for embroidery. Before attempting to digitize designs, become very familiar with the embroidery process.

If you are interested in digitizing, it is important to become familiar with how a design is stitched onto fabric. As you embroider, watch the stitching process of designs digitized by professional companies. Study how the machine is programmed to stitch the design. The first series of stitches are called underlay stitches, which are a series of running stitches that lay the foundation of the design. Quality digitized designs should always have underlay stitches.

The fill stitches are next—whether satin or running, these stitches fill the design with color and make the motif come to life. The stitches that jump from color to color throughout a design are called "jump stitches". At the very end of a design or before a jump stitch, there are "tie off" stitches that stitch several times near each other to tie the thread. These are just some of many components that make up a quality embroidery design.

Once you become familiar with the embroidery process, use your product specific software to try digitizing a design. Check with your local embroidery equipment dealer for classes on digitizing.

Patricia D. A. "Patty" Reinert, embroidery technician/coordinator for Dakota Collectibles, says: "When stitching two or more parts in a design, it's important to follow a few simple steps to ensure successful alignment. Use a large hoop to accommodate the entire design. Just before you start the stitching process, write down the number where the needle is positioned and note the rotation of the design. Stitch the first part of the design. When the machine indicates the design is complete, do not cut the thread or remove the hoop from the machine. Select the second part of the design. Position the design according to the number you wrote down before stitching the first part. (Or, press the "pattern start key"—if it is an option on your machine.) The machine will move the needle to the first stitch of the second part, which should be directly over the last stitch. By not cutting the thread, there is no need to worry that lock stitches aren't present to secure the joined area. If you have automatic thread cutters on your machine, turn this option off for this process."

Embroidery designs from Cactus Punch.

Chapter 4

Creative Embroidery Techniques

Beyond basic embroidery lies the world of creative embroidery techniques. What you'll find in this chapter are the techniques that give new meaning to the words "creative machine embroidery". From cutwork to dimensional designs, these techniques will turn any project into a work of art.

Use the following basic embroidery supplies for each technique unless otherwise noted. It's important to only use quality products manufactured for embroidery machines. Keep a generous stock of your favorite brand(s) of basic products for use in every aspect of the embroidery process. This way you'll never be caught short of an essential item.

Basic Embroidery Supplies:
- Design appropriate for the technique
- Base fabric appropriate for the technique
- Stabilizer appropriate for the base fabric
- Temporary marking pen/pencil
- Embroidery machine needle—size appropriate for your fabric and thread
- Decorative embroidery thread
- Bobbin thread
- Hoop—smallest size for your design
- Hoop template
- Sharp, curved and straight blade scissors
- Spray adhesive
- Steam iron
- Padded ironing board

Janome design.

Cutwork

Sample of Cutwork; Elna design.

Cutwork is an embroidery technique in which the base material is cut-away to reveal the stabilizer. After the embroidery cutwork process, the stabilizer is removed to form smoothly stitched holes in the fabric. Allow your creativity to be your guide as to how much of the fabric is cut away within the design.

What you'll need
• Basic embroidery supplies (see page 55)
• Tightly woven base fabric
• Tear-away stabilizer (a light, easy-to-tear style)

Instructions:

1. Mark the placement of the design on your fabric and then hoop the fabric with the tear-away stabilizer.

2. Thread the machine and attach the hoop to the embroidery arm. Start the embroidery process; the machine will stop after stitching a double row of outline stitches.

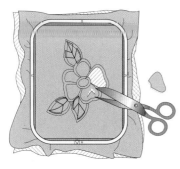

3. Remove the hoop from the machine; do not remove the fabric from the hoop. Trim the fabric only close to the inside stitching lines; do not trim away the stabilizer.

4. Re-attach the hoop to the machine and finish stitching the design.

5. When the design is complete, remove the hoop from the machine. Remove the fabric from the hoop and tear away the stabilizer; use tweezers to remove any excess stabilizer.

Optional method: Hoop the base fabric with a nylon organza. If necessary, use a spray adhesive to secure the two layers together before the hooping process. After the two outline stitches are embroidered, cut close to the base fabric—be sure to not cut through to the organza. Continue with the embroidery process until the design is complete. Place the embroidered piece on a glass cutting surface. On the glass surface, use a soldering iron to cut close to the stitches to remove the organza pieces. Clean finish the edges with the soldering iron, being careful not to burn the edges.

Lindee's tip: "I like to use a liquid, natural fiber solvent to dissolve fabric close to stitches when using cutwork designs—instead of trimming close to outline stitches. After stitching the outline stitches, I run a very fine line of the liquid solvent next to the stitches. Allow the solvent to dry or use a hair dryer to speed up the process. Once the liquid solvent is dry, continue the embroidery process until the design is complete. Remove the stabilizer and use a hot iron to disintegrate the fabric near the stitching. Don't worry the fabric should turn black and separate from the motif. Wash the fabric to remove any remaining black fibers."

Appliqué

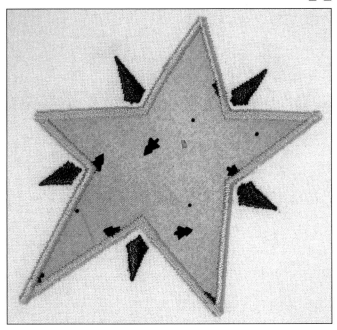

Sample of appliqué; Viking design.

Appliqué is the method of applying one fabric to the surface of another. The fabric is held down with satin or blanket embroidery stitches and can be used to replace a large area of fill stitches. There are several methods of appliqué—all of which are easy with the aid of your embroidery machine.

What you'll need:
- Basic embroidery supplies (see page 55)
- Tightly woven fabric for the appliqué fabric*
- Fusible or adhesive web designed for appliqué projects
- Paper scissors to cut out templates
- 4" x 6" index cards without lines
- Tape

*You can use just about any fabric as the appliqué. If you decide to use a knit fabric, stabilize the knit first with a piece of fusible tricot interfacing placed perpendicular to the stretch of the fabric. There are other types of fabrics that are suitable for appliqué such as organza, organdy, Polarfleece, interlock knit, satin, denim and more. A spray adhesive is an easy way to secure an appliqué fabric onto the base fabric.

Lindee recommends: "When selecting fabrics for appliqué, make sure the method of appliqué is compatible with your base fabric (i.e., Polarfleece, velvet, satin)."

Instructions for Designs Purchased with a Template

Some companies supply templates for the appliqué pieces. Here's how to appliqué using templates:

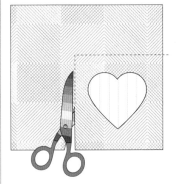

1. Trace the appliqué shape, using the supplied template, onto the paper of the fusible/adhesive web.

2. Cut the fusible/adhesive web larger than the traced shape.

3. Follow the manufacturer's instructions to apply the web to the wrong side of the appliqué fabric.

4. Cut out the appliqué shape following the lines drawn with the template on the web paper.

5. Mark the design placement on the base fabric and hoop the fabric with the appropriate stabilizer.

6. Thread the machine and attach the hoop to the embroidery arm. Start the embroidery process; the machine will stop after sewing the guide stitches in the shape of the appliqué design.

Continued on next page ➡

7. Remove the hoop from the machine; do not remove the fabric from the hoop. Secure the appliqué fabric within the guide stitches on the base fabric.*

8. Re-attach the hoop to the machine and finish stitching the design.

9. When the design is complete, remove the hoop from the machine.

10. Remove the fabric from the hoop and remove the stabilizer.

* An alternative method for securing the appliqué fabric to the base fabric is with a mini-iron called a "tacking iron". With the aid of an ironing board, iron the appliqué piece to the base fabric inside the hoop.

Instructions for Designs Purchased <u>without</u> a Template

Lindee says: "Some companies do not supply templates with their designs. Knowing how to make a template is useful even if your design comes with them. Supplied templates will not work if you scale the design. Here's how I make an appliqué template:"

1. Place the inner and the outer standard hoop pieces together without fabric and tighten the tension screw.

2. Tape a 4" x 6" index card to the backside of the hoops.

3. Thread the machine and attach the hoop to the embroidery arm. The machine will stitch the guide stitches for the appliqué onto the index card.

4. Remove the hoop from the machine and remove the index card from the hoop.

5. Cut the template out of the index card directly over the stitched lines.

6. Reset the machine to start and continue the embroidery process following the instructions for appliqué designs with a template.

Stitch & Trim Appliqué

This method is by far the quickest appliqué technique. However, it does require a bit of trimming accuracy. For best results, be sure to use a sharp, curved embroidery scissor for close trimming capabilities. Here's how to appliqué using the stitch and trim method:

Instructions:

1. Mark the design placement on the base fabric and hoop the fabric with the appropriate stabilizer.

2. Cut a 4" x 4" piece of fabric for the appliqué. Use a spray adhesive to secure the fabric for the appliqué to the hooped fabric.

3. Thread the machine and attach the hoop to the embroidery arm. Start the embroidery process; the machine will stop after stitching a guide stitch in the shape of the appliqué design. Remove the hoop from the machine; do not remove the fabric from the hoop.

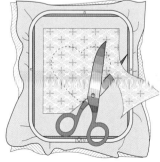

4. With a sharp curved pair of scissors, trim very closely to the outside edge of the guide stitch. Discard the excess fabric.

Lindee's tip: "When trimming, be very careful not to distort the fabric in the hoop. To prevent distortion, place the hoop on a flat surface. I like to use a notebook in my lap. If you hold the hoop in your hands your fingers may put too much pressure on the hooped fabric."

5. Re-attach the hoop to the machine and finish stitching the design. When complete, remove the hoop from the machine. Remove the fabric from the hoop and remove the stabilizer from the fabric.

Mary Mulari, an industry expert on all methods of appliqué and author of 10 books on the subject, says: "I like to use a spray adhesive to secure my appliqué fabric to the hooped base fabric. It's quick and it holds the fabric without it shifting during the embroidery process. I've had the best luck using a very sharp pair of curved scissors to trim the excess fabric. It is important to cut within 1/16" or less from the stitching line to prevent the fabric from poking through to the outside of the finishing satin or blanket stitches. "

Sample of reverse appliqué; Elna design.

Reverse Appliqué

Reverse appliqué is an embroidery technique much like cutwork. Instead a decorative fabric is placed between the base fabric and the stabilizer. After the stitching of the two rows of outlines stitches, the base fabric is cut-away to reveal the decorative material. This technique is similar to cutwork and the opposite of traditional appliqué.

Instructions:

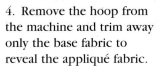

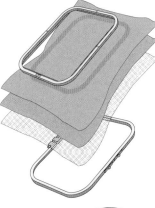

1. Refer to the cutwork supplies and instructions found on page 56.

2. Hoop the materials with the decorative fabric sandwiched between the base fabric and the tear-away stabilizer.

3. Start the embroidery process and stitch the two rows of outline stitches.

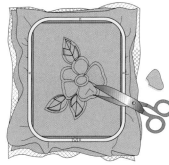

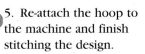

4. Remove the hoop from the machine and trim away only the base fabric to reveal the appliqué fabric.

5. Re-attach the hoop to the machine and finish stitching the design.

6. Remove the hoop from the machine and remove the fabric from the hoop. Tear away the stabilizer and trim away the excess appliqué fabric on the backside of the design close to the outside of the stitching.

Experiment using a sheer fabric behind the base fabric. The base fabric is cut away to expose the sheer fabric. The sheer fabric will add stability to the stitches that would otherwise be without support.

Double-sided Appliqué

Double-sided appliqué is an embroidery technique in which a piece of decorative fabric is stitched on the back and the front of the base material. Try this technique on reversible items such as towels or Polarfleece blankets with the same decorative thread in the bobbin and as the top thread. For best results, use appliqué fabrics that do not ravel, such as Ultrasuede® or Polarfleece. It is not advisable to use guide stitches with a satin-stitched appliqué finish since a stabilizer is not used with this technique. Therefore, use only the guide stitches or the guide stitches with a blanket stitch to clean finish the edges.

Instructions:

1. Hoop the base fabric and apply the appliqué fabric to the top and slide another piece of decorative fabric under the hooped fabric between the fabric and the bed of the machine.

2. Thread the machine and attach the hoop to the embroidery arm of the machine.

3. Start the embroidery process; the machine will stop after stitching a guide stitch in the shape of the appliqué design. It may be necessary to stitch twice around the design for added stability.

4. Remove the hoop from the machine; do not remove the fabric from the hoop.

5. Trim close to the design on both sides of the garment. If desired, re-attach the hoop to the machine to stitch the blanket stitches to complete the embroidery process.

Carol Bell, education consultant for Brother International, says: "The Brother International method for appliqué creates the appliqué piece directly from a piece of hooped decorative fabric. The Brother embroidery machine's appliqué designs are programmed to stitch two sets of guide stitches—one on the decorative fabric and the other on the base fabric. After the first set of guide stitches are made onto the hooped decorative fabric, remove the fabric from the hoop and cut out the appliqué design directly on the stitched line. Mark the design placement on the base fabric and hoop the fabric with the appropriate stabilizer. Attach the hoop to the embroidery arm of the machine and continue the embroidery process. The machine will stop after sewing the guide stitches in the shape of the appliqué design. Secure the appliqué to the fabric with a spray adhesive and continue the embroidery process."

Embroidery by Madiera.

Dimensional Embroidery

Sample of dimensional embroidery; Brother design.

Dimensional embroidery is a form of appliqué that has a 3-dimensional (raised) appearance when applied onto another base material. This technique has many purposes, one of which is for use on base fabrics that may not be suitable for embroidery—such as bridal satin, some velvet and delicate fabrics. After the stitching process, dimensional embroidery motifs can be machine sewn, pinned, snapped or buttoned onto another base fabric. Choose designs that have satin-stitched edges such as leaves, butterflies, flower petals or geometric shapes.

Dimensional embroidery motifs can be stitched onto a separate fabric just like an appliqué—by machine or by hand depending on the way in which the design will be used.

There are several ways to machine stitch the motif onto fabric. A single row of stitches down the center over previously embroidered stitches or with large zigzag stitches around the perimeter of the motif. Use clear monofilament thread or the same decorative thread to machine stitch the designs to the separate fabric. To stitch the design by hand, secure the design with pins on the right side of the fabric. From the reverse side of the fabric, thread a needle with coordinating thread and use long running stitches to secure the motif to the fabric being careful to catch the backside of the thickest parts of the motif onto the fabric. It may be necessary to continue checking the top of the motif in order to make sure the stitches are hidden.

What you'll need:

- Basic embroidery supplies (see page 55)
- Nylon fabric such as organdy or organza
- Soldering iron, wood burning tool or hot knife
- Sewing machine
- Sewing supplies

Instructions:

1. Hoop two layers of the nylon fabric perpendicular to each other.

2. Thread the machine and attach the hoop to the embroidery arm.

3. Start the embroidery process. When the design is complete, remove the hoop from the machine and remove the fabric from the hoop.

4. With sharp, straight embroidery scissors, trim very closely to the outside stitching line. Discard excess fabric.

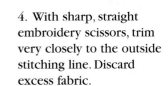

5. Use a soldering iron to swiftly touch and melt any remaining fabric between the cut edge and the stitching. Be swift as to not burn the fabric or stitching.

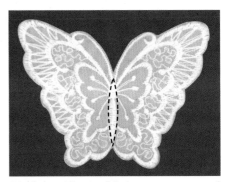

Stitch motif onto fabric near or around previously embroidered stitches.

Foam-

Linda McGehee, owner of Ghee's and author of Textures with Textiles *and* Simply Sensational Bags, *is the industry expert on texturizing fabric—from embroidery to thread painting. Her focus is the manipulation of embroidery designs into fabulous multi-dimensional works-of-art with an emphasis on flowers.*

Linda says, "The layering of stitched embroidery designs to create a multi-dimensional effect is perfect for use with flower petals and leafs. I like to stitch the designs on two layers of a sparkle organza in the hoop without a stabilizer. Depending on the look I am trying to achieve, I use some or all of a design. There are times when I only stitch the inside veins and the outline satin stitched parts of a design. There is a lot to be said for using a portion of a design—it can save valuable stitching time or offer a chance for the sparkle organza to glisten in the stitched motif."

Embroidered by Linda McGehee; Linda's Cactus Punch design.

Embroidered by Linda McGehee; Linda's Cactus Punch design.

"Try using two different colors of sparkle organza together—red and pink together are absolutely wonderful for poinsettia bracts."

"After the stitching is complete, I attach a unique decorative button or piece of jewelry in the center. On the backside, trim the Ultrasuede close to the stitching using appliqué scissors to protect the motif."

From Linda's Cactus Punch design disk.

"I like to layer and stitch my embroidered pieces onto layers of Ultrasuede. Thread the sewing machine with the same threads used to embroider the motif. Stitch the leaves and petals onto the Ultrasuede base using the previous embroidery as a guide. Stitch halfway down the center of the leaf or petal to offer a raised-effect to the flower."

See Fringing for more tips from Linda.

Foam-raised Embroidery

Sample of foam-raised embroidery; embroidery and design by Janome.

Foam-raised embroidery is a technique in which embroidery foam is used as a topping to lift the decorative threads off the base fabric. The threads are stitched over the foam to offer visual interest to the design. The embroidery needle self-cuts the foam for a clean finish. Foam adds stiffness to a design.

Therefore, choose fabrics and stabilizers appropriately. It is important to use designs that are digitized for foam. Be sure to test-stitch designs for compatibility with this technique. For best results, use satin-stitched designs that have minimal underlay stitches. It is important that the foam is not compressed before the satin stitches are embroidered.

What you'll need:
- Basic embroidery supplies (see page 55)
- Embroidery machine needle—ballpoint
- Cut-away stabilizer
- Embroidery foam

Instructions:

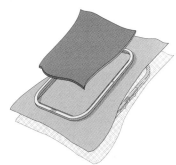

1. Mark the design placement on the base fabric and hoop the fabric with the appropriate stabilizer.

2. Thread the machine and attach the hoop to the embroidery arm. Place a piece of foam on top of the hooped fabric in the location where the design will stitch the pattern. It may be best to use a piece of foam the size of the hoop.

3. Start the embroidery process; the machine will stitch directly over the foam. The needle penetrations will puncture the foam for a clean finish. There may be only a portion of the design requiring the foam topping. Therefore, remove the excess foam from the hooped fabric as soon as the area of the design is complete.

Lacework

Sample of lacework; Brother design.

Lacework is an embroidery technique that involves the stitching of threads onto water-soluble base stabilizer, netting or sheer fabric to make a lace appliqué. The completed motif is applied onto another base fabric for decorative purposes. A lace design must be digitized to form a foundation of stitches that keep the decorative stitches in their correct form during the embroidery process. After the design has been stitched and the stabilizer is removed, the motif must hold its shape with the base stitches serving as the foundation. If the design cannot support the stitches alone, use a piece of netting or sheer fabric between the layers of water-soluble stabilizer.

What you'll need:
- Basic embroidery supplies (see page 55)
- 2 Pieces of water-soluble stabilizer (heavy weight)
- Embroidery machine needle—ballpoint
- Light-weight decorative thread in the machine needle and the bobbin
- English netting or sheer organdy (optional)
- Sewing machine
- Sewing supplies

Instructions:

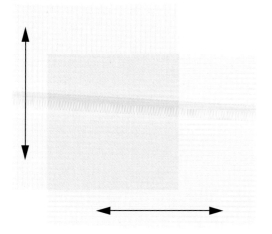

1. Hoop two layers of heavyweight, water-soluble stabilizer perpendicular to each other. Note that more layers may be needed depending on the amount of needle penetrations (the stitch count). Should the stabilizer be torn away during the test-stitch, add more layers of stabilizer. It may be necessary to use a piece of netting or sheer fabric between the layers of water-soluble stabilizer to hold the stitches of the design.

2. Wind the bobbin and thread the machine with the same color lightweight thread.

3. Attach the hoop to the embroidery arm.

4. Start the embroidery process and continue until the motif is complete.

5. Remove the hoop from the machine and remove the material from the hoop.

6. Tear away the stabilizer from the motif. If netting or organza was used to hold the stitches, clean finish the edges of the motif.

7. Rinse the motif under warm water to remove the stabilizer.

Do this several times to clear the residue from the motif. Allow the design to air dry to prevent shrinkage. Lightly press the motif, if necessary. Attach the lace motif to another fabric using the dimensional embroidery method found on page 61.

Lindee says: "I've had success using a heat-away stabilizer instead of a water-soluble when stitching lace designs. This type of stabilizer does not break down and holds the design together during the embroidery process. Heat the back of the motif until the stabilizer turns black. Sweep away the black charred remains and you'll be left with a perfectly-stitched lace motif."

Tonal Embroidery

Sample of tonal embroidery; Baby Lock design.

Tonal embroidery is a technique in which designs are stitched with one color of thread that blends with the base fabric color (also known as Tone-on-Tone embroidery). Whether designs are stitched onto fabric with a thread that is a shade lighter or darker than the fabric, you'll be amazed at the dramatic differences thread color tones can offer. Let your personal preference be your guide.

Tonal embroidery is best stitched with a high sheen thread that can offer a visible difference between the design, thread and fabric. Consider embroidery designs digitized for one color, but keep in mind that your selection may be limited.

Therefore, try designs that are digitized for cutwork and designs with multiple color changes. Multiple color designs are spectacular when stitched in all one color of thread—especially designs with textured stitching.

What you'll need:
• Basic embroidery supplies (see page 55)

Instructions:
1. Mark the design placement on the base fabric and hoop the fabric with the appropriate stabilizer.

2. Thread the machine and attach the hoop to the embroidery arm of the machine.

3. Start the embroidery process and continue with the same thread until the design is complete.

If your machine stops for a color change, start it up again without changing the thread. Some embroidery machines offer the feature of eliminating the stop between color changes. Refer to your user's guide for more information on this feature.

Embroidered Fabric

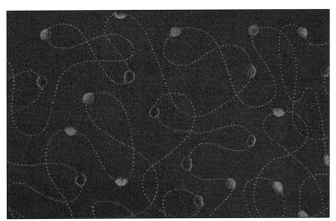

Sample of an all-over embroidered fabric; Viking design.

Embroidered fabric can be made by stitching several designs together to create an area of embroidered material. The material is then used to construct a garment or a portion of a garment. The secret to making embroidered fabric is to only stitch the fabric sections needed for a project.

Choose patterns that can cover small fabric areas. For quick results, use one color of thread to speed up the embroidery process.

What you'll need:
- Basic embroidery supplies (see page 55)
- Melt-away stabilizer
- Iron on a low setting (no steam)

Instructions:

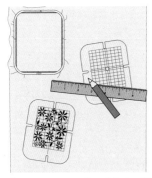

1. Determine the size of the fabric needed for the embroidered piece of fabric. Cut a piece of the base fabric substantially larger than needed for the project. Use a design alignment and template making method found in Chapter 3 to mark the first design placement on the fabric. Mark a continued line down and across the fabric to aid in next several hoopings. It may be necessary to continue marking the fabric after the first design is stitched. Hoop the fabric with the appropriate stabilizer. Thread the machine and attach the hoop to the embroidery arm.

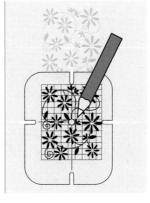

2. Start the embroidery process. After the design is complete, remove the hoop from the machine and remove the fabric from the hoop. Remove the stabilizer from the fabric. Use a template of the design to align and mark the fabric for the next hooping.

3. Re-hoop the fabric with the appropriate stabilizer. Be sure to align the hoop with marked fabric. Continue the embroidery process until the entire area of fabric is covered for the intended project.

4. Cut the pattern pieces from the embroidered fabric and stitch the pattern following the manufacturer's instructions.

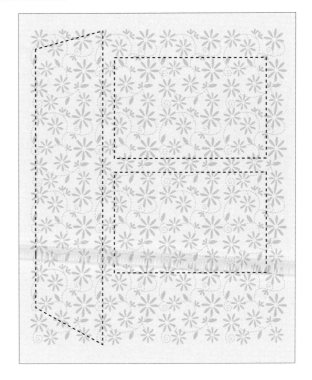

Texturizing Polarfleece

Embroidery on Polarfleece yields beautiful results with the proper stabilizers and specialty techniques. Designs stitched on this luscious fabric tend to imbed into the fabric, therefore use a water-soluble topping to keep the stitches on top of the fabric. Treat this fabric as you would any knit—stitch with ballpoint needles and a cut-away stabilizer.

Experiment with designs that have long stitches especially those that have satin stitches. Be sure to adequately stabilize designs to avoid cupping and added stiffness to this light fabric.

Texturizing Polarfleece is achieved by using light embroidery stitches or designs that hold down the fibers of the fleece. The underlay stitches of satin stitched designs make the best designs for texturizing Polarfleece. They are usually 3-step zigzag utility embroidery stitches and the first group of stitches that lay the foundation for the rest of the design. The underlay stitches stabilize the design area, secure the fabric to the stabilizer and hold the design in shape during and after the embroidery process. Look for designs specially digitized for this technique.

What you'll need:
- Basic embroidery supplies (see page 55)
- Embroidery machine needle—ballpoint
- Decorative embroidery thread—polyester or acrylic
- Water-soluble topping

Instructions:

This technique is just like making embroidered fabric and best used with a water-soluble stabilizer as a topping. Since a Polarfleece texturizing design is light and airy, there is no need for a stabilizer on the backside of the fabric.

1. Hoop the water-soluble topping with the fabric. Be sure to loosen the tension screw of your hoop dramatically to hold the fabric in place. The purpose of the hoop is to be a holder for the fabric and stabilizer.

2. After the embroidery process, remove the excess stabilizer and watch your fleece puff up around the design while the threads hold down the fibers of the fabric. This is a fun, easy way to add dimension to your solid Polarfleece fabrics.

Nancy Cornwell, author of Adventures in Polarfleece® *and* More Adventures in Polarfleece® *is the industry expert on fleece. Her next book, titled* Polar Magic *has a multitude of tips for embroidery on fleece.*

Nancy says, "Typically, a topping is used when embroidering stitched-filled motifs on lofty fabrics. However, to create texture on fleece eliminate the topping so that the stitches of an uncomplicated motif sink into the loft of the fabric. You'll want to achieve a contrast of depths in the fleece—stitched areas along with unstitched areas."

"Choose openwork designs and motifs that offer unstitched areas that puff-up between the stitched areas. Take advantage of your machine's fast-forward to skip past those embroidery steps you wish to eliminate. Use a soft, cut-away stabilizer to hold the design in shape while maintaining the contrast between the puffed-up areas and the stitched areas. Hoop the stabilizer, lightly spray the stabilizer with a spray adhesive, stick-on the fleece and embroider…without a topping."

Embroidery by Nancy Cornwell: design by Cactus Punch.

Other Techniques

There are so many wonderful techniques that can be achieved with an embroidery machine. Here are just a few more that will spark your interest with embroidery designs developed just for these techniques. Look for designs available for these techniques from your embroidery machine dealer or independent professional digitizing company.

Quilting

Embroidery machine quilting is a quick and easy alternative to traditional hand-stitched quilting. For ease in hooping, use a thin batting with two layers of traditional quilt fabric. Using your favorite piecing method, assemble the quilt. Mark the design placement on the fabric and hoop all the layers of the quilt together. Proceed with the embroidery process. Since this type of design is open and the fabric is stable, a stabilizer is not needed. Use a contrasting or matching color thread for the stitching—both yield the look of hand quilting with the ease of automatic embroidery machine quilting. If necessary, stitch the design several times to achieve the thickness of the quilting motif desired. Also, if you decide to use the motif as a design only, stitch the design onto fabric before piecing the quilt.

Sample of quilting; Janome design.

Lindee says: *"Quilting designs sew very quickly and are surprisingly versatile. Try combining several motifs to build a large medallion. Metallic threads make an elegant look. Or, try appliqué with quilting designs. This technique is great for fur, Polarfleece or other non-raveling fabrics. Simply cut a piece of material the size of the inner hoop, secure it to the base fabric, stitch in place and trim."*

Cross-stitch

Sample of cross-stitch embroidery; embroidery by Sudberry House.

The look of hand-stitch embroidery can be achieved with the aid of an embroidery machine and digitized designs. The method of cross-stitching by embroidery machine is best on loosely woven fabric such as linen or traditional cross-stitch cloth. Use a stabilizer that is appropriate for this type of fabric. When using traditional cross-stitch cloth, it is important to hoop the fabric on the straight of the grain. Use a water-soluble marker to draw a vertical and horizontal line indicating the grain lines of the fabric. Be sure the two lines intersect to form the center or start point of the design and match the hoop placement notches.

Fringing

Fringing is an embroidery technique in which unusually long digitized stitches are formed closely together and secured on one end by an area of short stitches. The bobbin threads of the long stitches arc clipped allowing the long stitches to be pulled to the surface forming securely looped threads. Fringing offers a wonderful texturizing effect to embroidery designs.

Sample of fringing; Viking design.

Linda McGehee, owner of Ghee's and the industry expert on dimensional embroidery, says: "I've had the best luck using a water-soluble thread in the bobbin to embroider designs with the fringing technique. After the design is stitched, I mist the back of the motif with water to allow the thread to disintegrate. Then, pull the decorative thread to the right side of the design for a perfectly fringed motif with a lot less bulk than the traditional method of clipping the bobbin threads."

"Be sure to change the bobbin from water-soluble thread to standard bobbin thread throughout the stitching of a fringed design. I'd suggest dedicating a bobbin to water-soluble thread by marking the bobbin with a permanent marker as a reminder that the thread is water-soluble. Should you forget that a water-soluble bobbin is in the machine when stitching a new design—you'll have quite a surprise after the first washing when you discover the design is gone and a pile of threads are in the bottom of your washer! Keep water-soluble thread and bobbins in airtight containers. Empty film containers are just the right size to hold the thread spool and bobbin together."

See Dimensional Embroidery for more tips from Linda.

Sample of watercolor painting on embroidery; Brother design.

Cross Over (Mixed Media)

Cross-over embroidery (sometimes referred to as mixed media) is the technique that involves using another craft form with the stitching of decorative designs. The combining of different art mediums can bring together many hobbies into one project. Try combining embroidery designs with stenciling, painting and ribbon embroidery to framed artwork, pillows, and garments.

Chapter 5

Embroidery Projects

These quick and easy projects were created to help utilize the techniques and information found in Chapters 1 through 4. Several of the projects use the decorative designs found on the CD located on the back cover of this book. The projects can be used with any decorative design. Therefore, if you do not have a computer and the software appropriate for your machine to utilize these designs, substitute the listed design in the projects for one from your own collection.

To use the designs on the disk, insert the CD into a computer. An installation page will automatically load onto the screen. From this page, select "Load Designs" and follow the instructions on each screen to install the designs onto the hard-drive of the computer. Be sure to load the designs in your brand-specific embroidery machine's format. Once the designs are on the computer, transfer the designs to the embroidery machine following the manufacturer's instructions for your embroidery equipment. For more information, consult the owner's manual or seek advice from the dealer who honors your equipment warranty.

There's always more than one way to utilize a decorative design. All multicolored digitized designs have stops programmed into the design, which can indicate a color change or a separation in a design. At each stop, consider how the design would look stitched with just those series of stitches. Look at all the possibilities built into one single motif for the opportunity to expand your library of designs.

Nicky Bookout, freelance instructor and designer for Bubbles Menagerie, says: "Remember…people see you both coming & going—put a little something on the back, too!"

Be sure to test-stitch all designs and techniques on fabric the same as or similar to the project fabric (see test-stitching on page 48). If the design recommends a particular color, it is not necessary to use that exact color shade of thread. As with every aspect of embroidery, let your imagination be your guide! Use the following basic embroidery supplies for each project unless otherwise noted.

Basic Embroidery Supplies:
- Design appropriate for the project
- Fabric or purchased item appropriate for the technique
- Stabilizer appropriate for the fabric or purchased item
- Temporary marking pen/pencil
- Embroidery machine needle—size appropriate for the project and thread
- Decorative embroidery thread
- Bobbin thread
- Hoop—smallest size for the design
- Hoop template
- Sharp, curved, and straight blade scissors
- Spray adhesive
- Steam iron and padded ironing board

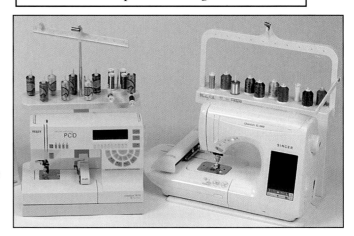

Some of the projects require simple straight stitch sewing techniques. When using a home embroidery and sewing machine, change the machine from embroidery to the sewing mode. If you're just getting started sewing or are interested in trying, consider taking a beginning sewing class. Basic sewing is an essential life skill. If you do not have access to a sewing machine, the projects can also be stitched by hand using a simple running stitch with a hand-sewing needle and thread.

Project 1: Celebrating with Cards

Tri-fold card from Paper Creations and decorative design from Dakota Collectibles.

Cards are a great way to use successful test-stitch samples from your design collection. Purchase special blank cards that are tri-folded with a cutout perfect for placement of embroidery designs. Decorate the outside of the card before starting the assembly process with rubber stamps for added personalization.

What you'll need:
- Basic embroidery supplies (see page 72)
- Test-stitch embroidery design stitched onto fabric
- Very thin batting (1/8")
- Tri-fold specialty window card and envelope
- Matching sewing thread
- Sewing machine
- Sewing supplies
- Topstitching needle
- Fabric glue stick (optional)
- Paper glue stick
- Light tear-away stabilizer

Instructions:

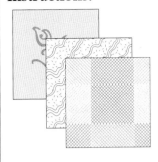

1. Measure the card while it is still folded. Cut a piece of the batting and stabilizer slightly smaller than the card measurement. Choose a test-stitch design appropriate for the size opening on the card and stitch it out.

2. On the wrong side of the fabric, center the batting and stabilizer pieces over the design. Cut the fabric the same size as the other pieces.

3. Use a spray adhesive to secure the fabric, batting and stabilizer pieces together.

4. Decorate the outside of the card window opening with stickers, rubber stamps or any art form prior to the assembly process.

5. To assemble the card, open up the card onto a flat surface. Place the layered fabric pieces behind the window opening of the card—make sure the design is centered inside the hole on the card. If necessary, use a fabric glue stitch to secure the fabric to the card.

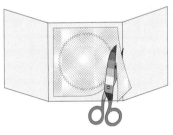

6. Using a sewing machine set for a 4-mm x 4-mm zigzag stitch, secure all the layers together by stitching directly onto the front of the card around the hole as illustrated.

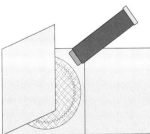

7. When complete, turn to the backside of the card and remove the tear-away stabilizer, trim the batting and the fabric within 1/2" - 1" from the stitching.

8. Use a glue stick to secure the front card lining to the backside of the decorated front section of the card.

Project 2: Gift Bag

CD from Brother; design by Amazing Designs.

Giving gifts is just as fun as wrapping them, especially with a custom made embroidered bag. Embroider it, stitch it and snap it for fun gift giving pleasure all year round! This is another project idea for using successful test-stitch samples.

What you'll need:

- Basic embroidery supplies (see page 72)
- (2) Pieces of fabric larger than the present
- Measuring tape
- Matching sewing thread
- Sewing machine
- Sewing supplies
- Reversible snap set(s)

Instructions:

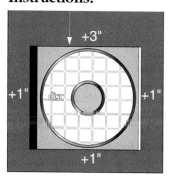

1. Place the gift on a flat surface. Measure the gift and allow for at least 1" extra fabric for the two sides and the bottom. Allow for 3" at the top for the fold and snap placement.

Note: If the gift is not flat, use a measuring tape to measure the circumference and add the above measurements.

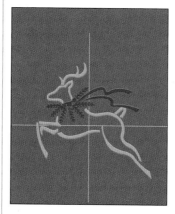

2. Cut two pieces of the fabric according to the measurements. On one half of the fabric piece, embroider the design in the center of the fabric. If the gift bag is small, it may be necessary to use the hoopless embroidery method found on page 47.

stitch 1/4" seam

3. With right sides together and a 1/4" seam, stitch the sides and bottom of the bag.

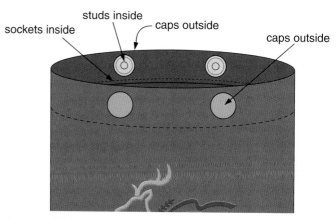

sockets inside studs inside caps outside caps outside

4. Turn right sides out and fold a 1" hem at the top and stitch a 3/4" hem. Attach the snap(s) according to the manufacturer's instructions as illustrated.

Project 3: Scented Sachet

Embroidery design from Elna.

If you enjoy accents that smell as pretty as they look, here's an embroidery project that can be filled with soap, potpourri, or scented beads. Use the reverse appliqué method on page 59 with a layer of sparkle organza and a cutwork design. A great idea for those who travel—helps to keep clothes smelling fresh inside a closed suitcase.

What you'll need:
- Basic embroidery supplies (see page 72)
- (2) Pieces of stable woven fabric 10" x 12" or pieces substantially larger than the hoop
- (1) Piece of sheer sparkle organza 10" x 12" or piece substantially larger than the hoop
- Matching sewing thread
- Sewing machine
- Sewing supplies
- Light tear-away stabilizer
- Soap, potpourri or scented beads
- Ribbon or cording

Instructions:

1. Using a design appropriate for cutwork and the reverse appliqué instructions found on page 59, sandwich the piece of sparkle organza between one of the two pieces of stable woven fabric and the stabilizer.

2. Locate the placement, hoop, and embroider the design onto the fabric.

3. Depending on the size bag needed for the project (larger for the potpourri and smaller for the beads, cut the fabric down to size using the Gift Bag instructions found on page 74. Follow the Gift Bag assembly instructions except press and stitch a double 1/4" hem for the top of Scented Sachet.

4. Insert the soap, potpourri or scented beads and tie the sachet with a decorative ribbon or cording.

Project 4: Pretty Pocket

Design from the CD included with this book.

These mini pockets are made completely on the embroidery machine. This unique technique combines appliqué with dimensional embroidery to create a functional pocket. Stitch the embroidered flower design that comes with the pocket or substitute it for a design of your own. You can even bypass making the pocket and use the flower design all by itself. This is an example of using a design to its fullest potential!

What you'll need:

- Basic embroidery supplies (see page 72)
- Embroidery design on the included CD
- Sewn or purchased item
- Fabric for the pocket the size of the inner hoop
- Matching sewing thread
- Sewing machine
- Sewing supplies
- 10" x 12" Nylon stabilizer, organdy or organza
- Soldering iron

Instructions:

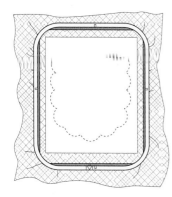

1. Hoop the nylon stabilizer, organdy or organza. Make your own adhesive stabilizer by following the instructions found on page 48. Spray the adhesive onto the nylon material and then secure the pocket fabric in the hoop.

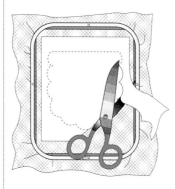

2. Start the embroidery process; the machine will stop after stitching a guide stitch in the shape of the pocket. Remove the hoop from the machine; do not remove the fabric from the hoop. Trim close to the stitching on the outside of the pocket to remove the excess fabric.

3. Re-attach the hoop to the machine and continue the embroidery process until the design is complete. Remove the hoop from the machine and remove the fabric from the hoop. Trim the stabilizer or organdy close to the outside stitching of the pocket.

4. Use a soldering iron to melt away the excess fabric from the pocket edges.

Fold Line

Fold

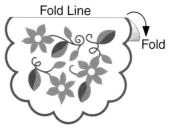

5. Fold down the top of the pocket toward the wrong side of the fabric at the fold line 1" from the top of the pocket.

6. Using a low-temperature iron setting, press the hem and design. Make multiple pockets, if necessary. Position the pocket on the sewn or purchased item; pin in place. Use a sewing machine to topstitch the pocket onto the fabric close to the inside edge of the pocket as illustrated.

76

Project 5: Personalized Pillowcase

Embroidery fonts from Cactus Punch.

From elegant monograms to child-like embroidered designs, a pillowcase is a wonderful canvas for many creative ideas. Super simple to stitch from scratch, pillowcases make gift-giving fun all year round. For a warm and cozy pillowcase, try making it out of solid-colored Polarfleece fabric.

What you'll need:

- Basic embroidery supplies (see page 72)
- Embroidery, monogram or lettering designs
- A 27" x 43" piece of decorative fabric
- A 10" x 43" piece of solid fabric
- Matching sewing thread
- Sewing machine
- Sewing supplies

Instructions:

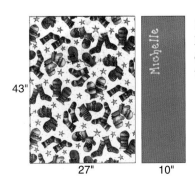

1. For a standard size pillowcase, mark and embroider the name onto the fabric as illustrated.

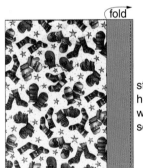

stitch header with 1/4" seam

stitch 1/4" seam

2. Once the embroidery is complete, fold the header in half with wrong sides together. Align raw edges together at one of the 43" edges of the decorative fabric and stitch using a 1/4" seam.

wrong side

fold

3. Fold the case in half with right sides together as illustrated. Stitch the remaining raw edges together using a 1/4" seam. Turn the case right sides out.

Project 6: Quickie Quilt

Brother embroidery designs; constructed by Christine VanHagen.

Here's a fun quilt project that's quick to stitch and makes the perfect canvas to display stitched designs from your collection. This project can offer the ability to use your embroidery equipment to machine quilt the layers together. Or, you can embroider the solid-colored squares with any design first and then construct the quilt using traditional methods. Consult your favorite quilt-making book for hints and tips along the way.

What you'll need:

- Basic Embroidery supplies (see page 74)
- Quilting embroidery design
- (6) 6 1/2" squares of white or cream 100% cotton quilt piecing fabric
- (4) 1-1/2" x 6-1/2" strips of coordinating 100% cotton quilt piecing fabric
- (1) 1-1/2" x 20-1/2" strip of coordinating 100% cotton quilt piecing fabric

- (2) 3" x 13-1/2" strips of coordinating 100% cotton quilt piecing fabric
- (2) 3" x 25" strips of coordinating 100% cotton quilt piecing fabric
- 20" x 30" piece of muslin for the backing
- Matching sewing thread
- Sewing machine
- Sewing supplies
- Very thin batting (1/8"—1/4")
- Tear-away stabilizer appropriate for the fabric (optional)

Instructions:

There are two ways to make this quilt. One, assemble the entire quilt and then embroider the quilt designs onto all the layers. Or two, embroider the squares of fabric and then assemble the quilt. Both ways are acceptable, depending on the embroidery designs used.

Method One

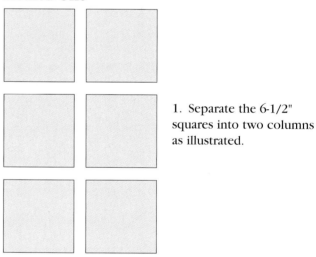

1. Separate the 6-1/2" squares into two columns as illustrated.

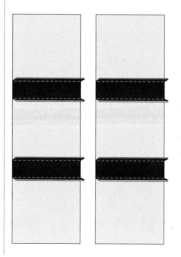

2. Using a 1/4" seam, stitch the four 1-1/2" x 6-1/2" strips to the bottom and/or top of the squares as illustrated.

78

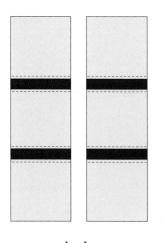

3. Press the seam allowances toward the strips.

7. On a clean, flat surface layer the backing, batting and the quilt top as illustrated. Pin the quilt together through all layers for stability. Finish using your favorite quilting method.

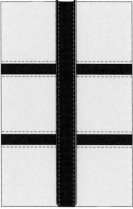

4. Using a 1/4" seam, stitch the one 1-1/2" x 20-1/2" strip to the left and right column as illustrated. Press the seam allowances toward the strips.

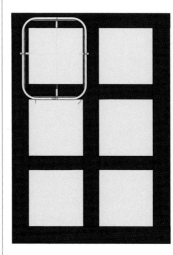

8. After the quilt is complete, mark the quilt where the embroidery designs are to be stitched. Hoop all the layers together without a stabilizer— the hoop functions as a holder, while the embroidery machine stitches the design. Embroider the designs onto the quilt. Repeat for each marked location.

5. Using a 1/4" seam, stitch the two 3" x 25" strips to both sides as illustrated. Press the seam allowances toward the strips.

Method Two

Hoop and embroider each of the six squares of fabric using a tear-away stabilizer. Follow the above steps to assemble the quilt. Then secure the layers together using your favorite quilting method.

6. Using a 1/4" seam, stitch the two 3" x 13-1/2" strips to the top and bottom as illustrated. Press the seam allowances toward the strips.

Project 7: Terrific Towels

Design from the CD in this book and lettering from Viking Sewing Machines.

Personalizing towels, with or without a name, can make quick and easy decorative additions to any bathroom. Experiment with lettering by embroidering "Family" for towels that are used by family members when guests arrive. Embroider the words "Face," "Hand" or "Bath" on corresponding towels for kids as they start becoming independent.

What you'll need:
- Basic embroidery supplies (see page 72)
- Embroidery design on the included CD
- Purchased towels
- Adhesive stabilizer
- Water-soluble or coordinating vinyl topping stabilizer

Instructions:

1. Using the placement guidelines found on page 40, locate and mark the placement of the design. Using the hoopless embroidery method (see page 47), secure the towel to the stabilizer.

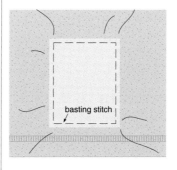

2. Secure the water-soluble or vinyl topping to the top of the towel with spray adhesive. Before the embroidery process, stitch a basting stitch around the outside parameter of the design.

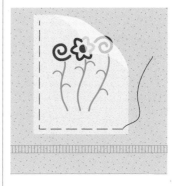

3. Embroider the design onto the towel. When the design is completed, remove the basting stitches, trim the threads and remove the stabilizer/topping. If a name will be added to the towel, repeat the above steps to stitch the name or monogram below the embroidered motif.

Project 8: Polar Pillow

Embroidery designs from Cactus Punch.

This project uses the Texturizing Polarfleece technique found on page 67. Use the embroidery machine hoop as a holder to embroider the fleece for this travel pillow cover that's a snap to stitch-up!

What you'll need:
- Basic embroidery supplies (see page 72)
- Polarfleece fabric piece (25" x 25")
- Matching sewing thread
- Sewing machine
- Sewing supplies
- Travel Pillow Form (12" x 16")
- (10-12) Reversible Long-Prong Snaps
- Water-soluble stabilizer for the topping

Instructions:

1. Follow the instructions on page 67 to texturize the Polarfleece fabric piece.

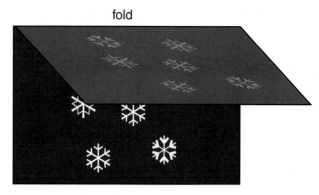

fold

2. To construct the pillow cover, fold the fabric piece lengthwise with right sides together. Be sure to match the cut edge.

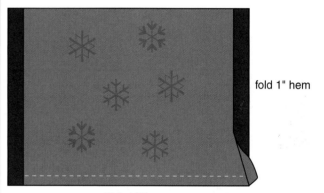

fold 1" hem

stitch 1/4"

3. Stitch the length of the fabric with 1/4" seam. Fold and stitch a 1" hem at each end.

reversible closure

caps outside

socket/stud inside

4. Turn the pillow cover right sides out. Attach reversible snap sets according to the manufacturer's instructions 3" from the opening on both sides of the pillow cover. Be sure to use the correct snap components as illustrated.

5. Insert the pillow form and snap the ends closed.

Project 9: Super Project Saver

Embroidery designs from Elna.

What happens when a project doesn't turn out the way you anticipated or perhaps suffered a mishap due to an embroidery complication? Use this project technique to save an item that might have otherwise ended up in the recycle bin. Here's yet another project to utilize successful test-stitch samples.

What you'll need:
- Basic embroidery supplies (see page 72)
- Sewn or purchased item with an embellished mishap
- Test-stitch sample on a color-coordinating woven fabric or color-coordinating woven fabric substantially larger than the area to fix
- Fusible tricot knit interfacing
- Matching sewing thread
- Sewing machine
- Sewing supplies

Instructions:

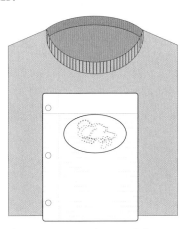

1. Determine the geometric shape of the area to be fixed. For example, is the original design square or circular or more oval? Trace the shape of the determined geometric shape onto a sheet of paper. Be sure the geometric shape is at least 1/2" larger on all sides to cover up the entire design area. Cut the shape out of the paper.

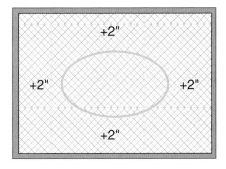

2. Cut a square of the woven fabric 2" larger on all sides of the area to be fixed. Repeat for the fusible tricot knit interfacing. Fuse the interfacing to the wrong side of the blank fabric square. Using a temporary marking pen/pencil, trace the paper shape onto the interfaced side of the fabric.

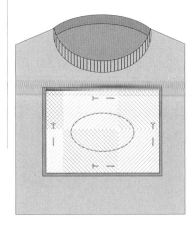

3. Pin the square onto the right side of the fabric directly over the original design. Stitch the square directly over the marked shape; be sure to completely encase the original design.

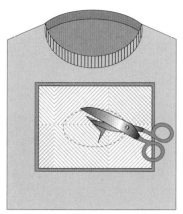

4. Using a sharp scissors, clip through the center and trim 1/8" from the stitched geometric shape.

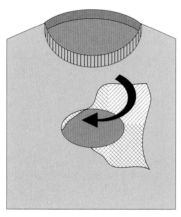

5. Turn the facing to the wrong side of the opening. On the backside of the project with the facing toward you, use an iron to press the opening. While pulling lightly on the square, be sure to roll the fabric slightly inward toward the facing square.

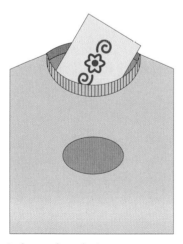

6. Specially stitch another design onto woven fabric or use a test-stitch sample no larger that the size of the opening. Cut a piece of interfacing the size of the fabric and interface the backside of the fabric over the back of the design. Center the design on the backside of the fabric through the opening in the project. Make sure the design is centered in the opening. Pin in place.

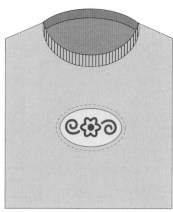

7. On the right side of the fabric, stitch the new fabric piece into place 1/2" from the opening through all the layers (the top layer of the project, the opening fabric and the design fabric).

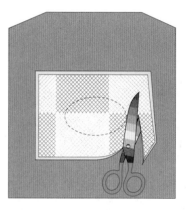

8. On the inside, trim both layers within 1" to 1-1/2" from the last stitching line.

Project 10: Simply Sensational Sheers

Instructions:

Brother embroidery design.

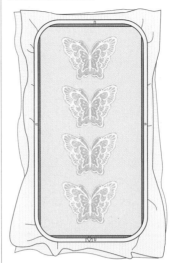

1. Follow the dimensional embroidery instructions found on page 61 to embroider butterflies onto two layers of organza. Use an extra large hoop to embroider the butterflies as many times as possible within the hoop.

2. After the embroidery process, trim away the excess fabric very close to the stitching of each butterfly. Using a soldering iron, quickly touch the iron to the outside edge of the fabric to melt away any remaining fabric close to the stitching. Pin the butterflies in random placements on the sheers as illustrated.

Purchase sheer drapes, add some dimensional butterfly embroideries and you'll have some simply sensational sheers. Use the dimensional embroidery technique found on page 61 to embroider butterflies onto sheer nylon organdy. Randomly stitch them onto the sheer drapes and you'll have butterflies aflutter all year round!

What you'll need:
- Basic embroidery supplies (see page 72)
- Purchased sheer drapes
- Matching sewing thread
- Sewing machine
- Sewing supplies
- Extra large hoop
- Soldering iron

3. Stitch on both sides of the butterfly body for each motif using thread the same color as the butterfly. If more butterflies are needed, repeat the embroidery process.

Project 11: Patch Perfection

Design from the included CD.

This dual appliqué patch, with a hint of fall splendor, is perfect for projects from pillows to garments. Stitch the motif as a patch or directly onto an item—you can even stitch the design without the appliqué fabrics for added contrast. The beauty of this design is that it can be masculine or feminine depending on the colors chosen for the thread and the appliqué.

What you'll need:
- Basic embroidery supplies (see page 72)
- Embroidery design on the included CD
- Purchased or sewn item
- (2) 4" x 4" pieces of fabric for the appliqué
- A piece of washable felt the size of the inner hoop for the patch base
- Sewing machine
- Sewing supplies
- Matching sewing thread
- Adhesive stabilizer
- Nylon stabilizer or sheer organdy (optional)
- Soldering iron (optional)

Instructions:

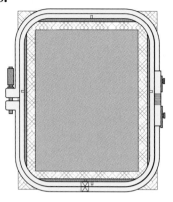

1. Using the hoopless embroidery method found on page 47, secure the piece of washable felt to the stabilizer.

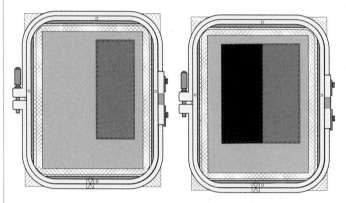

2. Use an appliqué method of your choice from pages 57 to secure both the right and left appliqué fabric pieces to the base fabric.

3. After the appliqué fabrics have been stitched to the base fabric, continue with the embroidery process until the design is complete.

85

4. When the embroidery process is complete, remove the felt from the adhesive stabilizer. Trim the felt up to 1/4" away from the outside edge of the stitching.

For an alternative idea, hoop two pieces of nylon organdy perpendicular to each other to form the base fabric. Using the instructions above stitch the entire design. After the design is stitched and the excess fabric is trimmed away, use a soldering iron to melt the nylon close to the stitching to create a flangeless patch. With a needle and thread, whip-stitch the patch onto the fabric from the wrong side of the garment. This particular garment has two different textures of fabric and an intersecting seam, which makes it impossible to stitch this motif directly onto the fabric. Therefore, making a patch was the perfect solution to embellish this garment.

5. Using a sewing machine and matching thread, stitch the patch onto the sewn or purchased item.

Project 12: Framed for You!

Design from the included CD.

Framing designs is one of my favorite projects. You can purchase framing supplies at your local arts & craft supply store in any quantity, size, and shape. Or, you can have your designs professionally framed at an art studio. Experiment with photo frames that have sections to highlight several sizes of designs in one frame. Combine designs to create a masterpiece that can be mounted in a large frame. Add glass or leave it open—creative framing can show off your works of embroidery art! Here's another project for utilizing test-stitch samples.

What you'll need:
- Basic embroidery supplies (see page 72)
- Frame
- Embroidery design(s) stitched onto fabric larger than the frame
- Adhesive needlework mounting board
- Measuring tape
- Hammer
- Frame pins
- Rotary cutting supplies

Instructions:

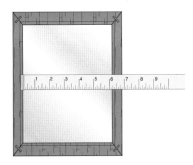

1. Measure the inside dimensions of the frame.

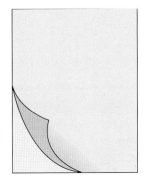

2. Cut a piece of adhesive needlework mounting board the size of this measurement and peel back the adhesive.

3. Secure the embroidered fabric onto the board. Make sure the design is centered in the frame. Smooth out the fabric and trim the fabric to the exact size of the board.

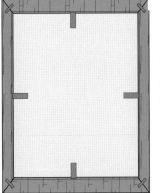

4. Place the board into the frame. With a hammer, secure the frame pins to the frame flange to hold the board in place.

Project 13: Practical Purse

Design from Viking.

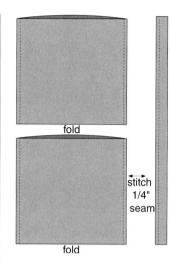

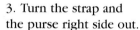

2. Cut a piece of fabric 40" x 2-1/2" for the strap and fold all pieces in half. With right sides together and a 1/4" seam, stitch the side seams of the purse, lining and strap as illustrated. Press the seams open.

stitch 1/4" seam

fold

fold

3. Turn the strap and the purse right side out.

Here's a purse that's functional, yet easy to stitch. Make several for each season—a great way to experiment embroidering on a variety of fabrics.

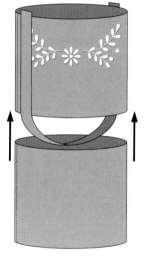

4. Position the strap on the outside of the purse as illustrated (on opposite outside edges). Pin the lining over the strap and purse, as shown.

What you'll need:
- Basic embroidery supplies (see page 72)
- 1/3 Yard of fabric for the purse and lining
- Fusible interfacing (optional)
- Adhesive stabilizer
- (1) Button or reversible snap closure
- Matching sewing thread
- Sewing machine
- Sewing supplies
- Large safety pin

5. Stitch using a 1/4" seam—leave a 3" opening for turning.

Instructions:

1. Cut two pieces of fabric 8-1/2" x 18" for the purse and the lining. Depending on the weight of the purse fabric, it may be necessary to fuse a piece of interfacing to the wrong side of the purse fabric for added support. Use the hoopless embroidery method found on page 47 to hoop and embroider a curved design on the top and bottom of the fabric. Be sure to embroider the design no less than 1" from the top/bottom and side edges.

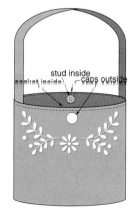

stud inside   caps outside

6. Turn the entire purse right sides out. Carefully press the edges. Hand stitch the opening closed. Top stitch the top around the entire opening. Use a button or snap as the closure.

Project 14: Pretty Pillow

Design from the included CD.

This design, found on the CD, features many elements that can be interchangeable. Stitch the motif with or without the appliqué fabric. Stitch the appliqué fabric alone. Use the roses in a dimensional embroidery project. Change the colors of the roses depending on who the project will given to—choose two different colors of yellow for friendship or two different colors of red for love. Make the pillow from a square or round pillow form or make a quilt with squares embroidered with different colors of roses. The possibilities are endless!

What you'll need:
- Basic embroidery supplies (see page 72)
- Embroidery design on the included CD
- 12" Round pillow form
- (2) 13" Round pieces for the base fabric
- 2 Strips of decorative fabric 3" x 13"
- (2) 4"x 4" pieces of fabric for the appliqué (optional)
- 3 Snap sets or buttons
- Matching sewing thread
- Sewing machine
- Sewing supplies

Instructions:

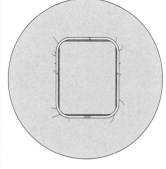

1. Mark the design placement on one of the two pieces of 13" round base fabric and hoop the fabric with the appropriate stabilizer.

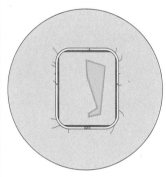

2. Use an appliqué method from pages **57** to embroider the appliqué fabric to the base fabric.

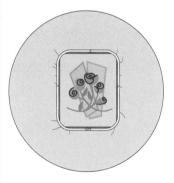

3. Continue the embroidery process until the motif is complete.

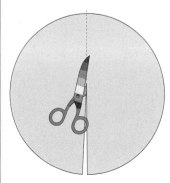

4. To construct the pillowcasing, cut the remaining 13" round piece in half.

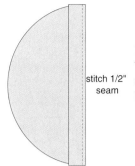

stitch 1/2" seam

5. Fold the 3" strips in half lengthwise. With right sides together and a 1/2" seam, stitch the strips onto both cut edges.

stitch 1/4" seam

7. With right sides together, pin the pillow pieces together and stitch using a 1/4" seam around the entire circle.

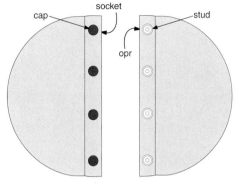

cap   socket   stud

opr

6. Attach snaps according to the manufacturer's instructions in the locations as illustrated.

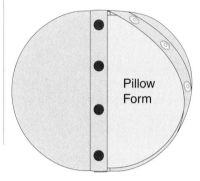

Pillow Form

8. Turn the pillow to the right sides through the snapped opening and insert the pillow form.

Project 15: Flower Power

Use a portion of the design from the included CD to embroider a hat.

Here's an idea for using a part of a design in a project. This design has 3 color changes—the stems, the outside of the flower and the curls. The curls and flowers are the design parts needed for this project. In addition, the curls and flowers are at an angle. It will be necessary to determine the angle of the flowers during the test-stitch process and compensate for the angle when stitching directly on the hat. In the beginning, it's an ingenuity test that once overcome, will be fun to repeat over and over again.

What you'll need:
• Basic embroidery supplies (see page 72)
• Embroidery design on the included CD
• Sewn or purchased Polarfleece hat
• Embroidery machine needle—ballpoint
• Adhesive stabilizer
• Additional cut-away stabilizer (optional)
• Water-soluble stabilizer

Instructions:

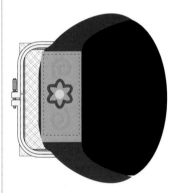

1. Using the hoopless embroidery method found on page 47, adhere the stabilizer to the backside of the hoop or use a frame hoop.

2. Mark the design placement on the hat and adhere the hat to the stabilizer inside the hoop.

3. Secure the water-soluble stabilizer as the topping over the fleece and baste. Stitch only the flowers; bypass stitching the stems. When the motif is complete, do not press the design—the Polarfleece cannot tolerate the heat of an iron.

Project 16: Kid Wrap

Embroidery design from Amazing Designs.

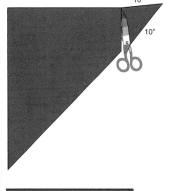

2. Measure 10" down the fold and the same on the cut or binding edge. Mark and cut the fabric between the two points as shown.

3. Pin and stitch the cut edge using a 1/4" seam.

Here's a quickie gift to make for a baby. It's made from a 1-1/4 yards square of Polarfleece. Fold, cut, stitch and embroider it to make a hooded baby cover-up perfect to keep your favorite bundle of joy warm. For bath time fun, make it from an oversized beach towel, too!

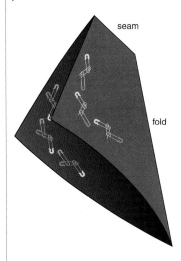

4. Embroider the two sides of the blanket or fabric from the corner to within 12" of the seam.

What you'll need:
- Basic embroidery supplies (see page 72)
- Sewn or purchased blanket, Polarfleece or towel at least 36" - 45" square
- Matching sewing thread
- Sewing machine
- Sewing supplies
- Bias binding (purchased or self-made)

Instructions:

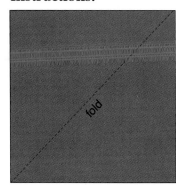

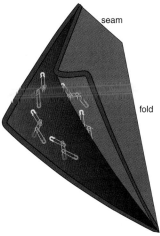

1. With right sides together, fold the square fabric or blanket in half to form a triangle.

5. If constructing the blanket from Polarfleece fabric, use a purchased or self-made binding to finish the edges at this time.

Project 17: Fancy Fabric Centerpiece

Design is from the included CD.

By making your own embroidered fabric, the project possibilities are endless. Here's an idea for making a simple table centerpiece. Be sure to make the fabric large enough to show off the embroidery around a floral arrangement, a lamp or a decorative candle. A variegated thread will provide subtle color variations in all-over designs.

What you'll need:
- Basic embroidery supplies (see page 72)
- Embroidery design on the included CD
- (1) 18" x 18" Piece of woven base fabric
- (4) 3" x 18" Strips of coordinating fabric
- (1) 16" x 16" Piece of woven fabric for the backing
- Matching sewing thread
- Sewing machine
- Melt-away stabilizer

Instructions:

1. Use the fabric making instructions found on page 66 to create the embroidered fabric. This technique will require 9 hoopings of the base material to create a 10-1/8" x 11-3/4" square of embroidered fabric. Trim the embroidered fabric to this size.

2. Using a 1/4" seam, sew a 3" strip to the top and bottom of the embroidered fabric. Trim excess fabric.

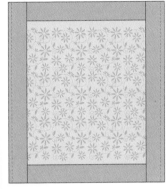

3. Using a 1/4" seam, sew a strip to both sides of the embroidered fabric. Trim excess fabric.

4. Cut the backing fabric the same size as the pieced top and place right sides together.

5. Using a 1/4" seam, stitch the pieced top and the backing pieces together. Be sure to leave a 3" opening for turning. Turn right sides out through the opening. On the backside, carefully press the seams flat to form the square. Hand stitch the opening closed.

Project 18: Switch 'n Stitch It

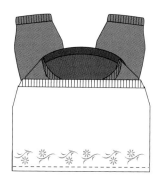

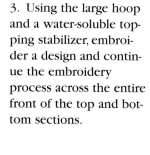

Embroidery design by Viking.

2. Draw a line horizontally 3"-4" from the cut line across the front of the upper and lower lightcolored sweatshirt as shown. Use these lines as your design placement guide.

3. Using the large hoop and a water-soluble topping stabilizer, embroider a design and continue the embroidery process across the entire front of the top and bottom sections.

4. After the embroidery process stitch the two sweatshirts together using a 1/4" seam.

Take two differently colored sweatshirts and horizontally cut them in half. Embroider the lightest-colored sweatshirt edges, switch and stitch them back up. Take advantage of the large opening for stitching on the top or bottom of the shirts. Use the hoopless embroidery method and Lindee's idea of utilizing the adhesive stabilizer as a hooping aid (page 47) by securing the stabilizer to the back of hoops, cutting a hole the size of the design, adhering a cut-away stabilizer over the hole and then embroider the design.

What you'll need:
- Basic embroidery supplies (see page 72)
- (2) Purchased sweatshirts (each one a different color)
- Embroidery machine needle—ballpoint
- Adhesive stabilizer
- Large hoop
- Cut-away stabilizer
- Water-soluble stabilizer

Instructions:

1. Cut the two sweatshirts horizontally in half.

Project 19: To Appliqué or not to Appliqué

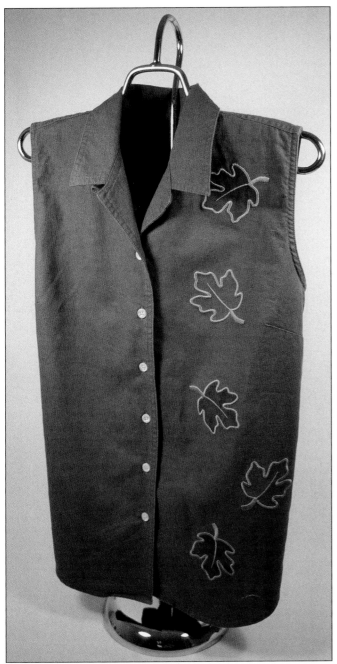

To appliqué or not to appliqué, that is the option! Randomly embroider tumbling leaves down the front of a shirt—applique some and just use the stitching for others. Here's a great lesson in creative random placement.

What you'll need:
- Basic embroidery supplies (see page 72)
- Sewn or purchased shirt
- Appliqué leaf designs
- Appliqué fabric

Instructions:
With the appliqué technique of your choice, randomly embroider leaves with and without appliqué fabric tumbling down a sewn or purchased top between the shoulder seam and the lower hemline. Be sure to use the correct hooping and stabilizing methods for the fabric being used.

Embroidery design Cactus Punch—Mary Mulari's Signature Disk.

Project 20: Patch It Up

Design from the included CD.

What you'll need:
- Basic embroidery supplies (see page 72)
- Embroidery design on the included CD
- Item of clothing with a hole (jeans)
- 4" x 4" Piece of bright-colored woven fabric (yellow)
- Seam ripper
- Matching sewing thread
- Sewing machine
- Sewing supplies
- Adhesive stabilizer
- Cut-away stabilizer

Instructions:

1. Turn the jeans inside out. Use a seam ripper to open an area on the flat-stitched seam large enough to insert the standard size hoop. Turn the jeans right sides out. Slide the hoop in between the layers.

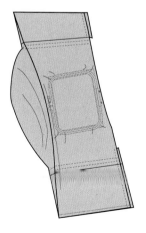

2. Secure the hooped stabilizer to the back of the jeans. The adhesive stabilizer will hold the torn fabric during the embroidery process. Be sure the fabric surrounding the area is moved away from the stitching area.

Here's a perfect idea for kids clothes. Use this project to repair holes in clothing—especially knees of jeans. Open up the side seam of the jeans to enable embroidery in this tight area of the pant leg. The fabric being embroidered will usually show through the lightning bolt and wheels. But, when used as a patch, a piece of fabric is used under the running stitches of the lightning bolt to cover up the hole. Use the hoopless embroidery method found on page 47 to assist with the embroidery process.

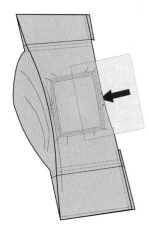

3. Slide a piece of cut-away stabilizer under the hoop between the bed of the machine and the bottom of the hoop. This stabilizer will protect the fabric from added wear. Start the embroidery process.

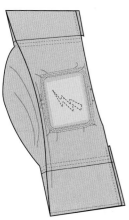

4. After stitching the flames behind the skateboard, the machine will stop (stop #3). Change to the next color of thread. Remove the hoop from the machine. Use spray adhesive to secure the bright-colored fabric to the jean material. Re-attach the hoop to the machine and stitch the outline of the lightning bolt. Be sure to stop the machine directly after stitching the lightning bolt and before it continues to stitch the remaining skateboard.

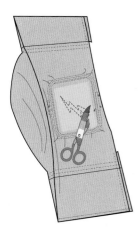

5. Remove the hoop from the machine and trim around the lightning bolt in the shape of an oval. Do not trim closer than a 1/4" from the stitching. Re-attach the hoop to the machine.

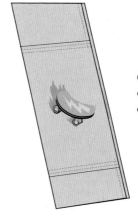

6. Continue with the embroidery process until the motif is complete.

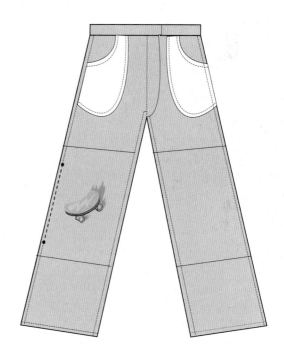

7. Turn the jeans inside out again. Using a sewing machine, stitch up the opening made in the seam.

Chapter 6

Inspirational Embroidery Showcase

hey say a picture says a thousand words. In the world of machine embroidery, this statement is not only true, but also visually inspirational. Here's a collection of projects from embroidery experts and suppliers across the industry to help spark your creative embroidery imagination.

Embroidery by Linda McGehee;
Embroidery Designs by Cactus Punch

Use Linda McGehee's technique of dimensional embroidery (see page 62) to layer embroidered leafs and petals for the creation of multi-dimensional flowers. Add a one-of-a-kind button or piece of jewelry to the center for an elegant wearable piece of art.

Photograph from Embroideryarts:
Embroidered and Sewn by Pauline Richards

Elegantly cover an address book with textured fabric and a single monogram embroidery motif from the Embroideryarts design collection. Here's yet another wonderful creation from Pauline Richards, editor of Total Embellishment Newsletter.

Photographs from Sulky of America; Embroidery designs by Amazing Designs; Embroidery by Sulky of America

Embroidery can bring all the colors of a quilt together. Here's a collection of embroidery designs on quilts using Joyce Drexler's Amazing Designs disk. Quilting is made easy with the aid of Joyce's book Secrets to Successful Quilting.

Photograph from Viking Sewing Machines

Embroider and sew up a Trick-or-Treat bag for Halloween with a ghoulishly fun embroidery design from Viking Sewing Machines.

Photographs from Sudberry House

Achieve the look of cross-stitch by hand using an embroidery machine and designs from the Sudberry House. These designs are digitized specifically to complement their brand of box collection, yet can be stitched on any project. For the most authentic appearance, embroider on traditional Aida cloth that is used for cross-stitch by hand.

Photographs from Viking Sewing Machines

Special occasion fabrics are easy to embroider with a bit of patience, fine embroidery needle and thread. For best results, reduce the embroidery speed when stitching onto this type of delicate fabric.

It's time for tea with this beautifully embroidered tablecloth. Measure and mark the circumference of the tabletop and stitch design randomly within this area.

Framed embroidery scenes make a wonderful wall hanging especially with bright sunflowers, bees and other pieces of nature.

Photographs from *SewNews* Magazine

Be sure to look for more creative ideas in publications such as Sew News, Creative Machine Embroidery, Arts & Crafts, Designs in Machine Embroidery, Embroidery Enthusiasts Magazine *and more. (See Resources starting on page 136)*

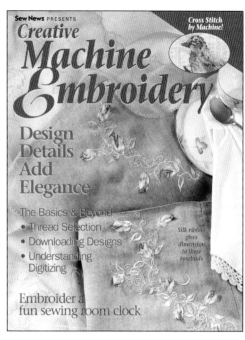

Photograph from Baby Lock USA; Embroidery Designs by Baby Lock

Delicate embroidery designs make beautiful accents on heirloom dresses. From christening to Sunday attire, be sure to use small, dainty designs specifically digitized for lightweight heirloom fabrics. Since heirloom fabric tends to be sheer, use a stabilizer that will not show through to the right side of the fabric.

Photographs from Viking Sewing Machines

Add some splash to a shower curtain or add embroidery to a diaper bag or stitch up a cluster of cats on a mini-quilt wall hanging by using one embroidery design disk from Viking Sewing Machines. Test your imagination to see how many different ways you can use designs from a multiple design disk!

Embroidery by Mary Mulari, Embroidery Designs by Cactus Punch

Stitch appliqué designs onto a silky scarf using sparkle organdy, water-soluble stabilizer and your favorite spray adhesive. For best results when hooping, sandwich the scarf between two layers of water-soluble stabilizer. Embroider the motifs using a fine embroidery needle and thread.

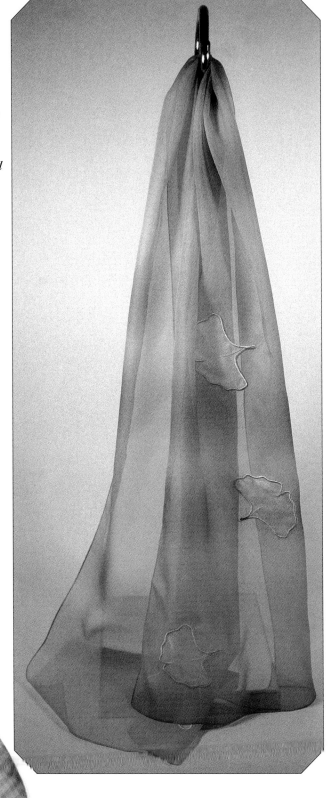

Photograph and Design from Sew Baby

This infant car seat cover makes the perfect canvas for baby motifs from your design collection. Be sure to center and embroider the fabric before sewing the cover.

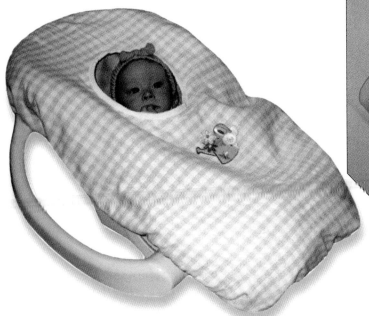

Embroidery and Designs from Dakota Collectibles

The front and back of this toddler sleeper is the perfect canvas for some fun embroidery designs from Dakota Collectibles. These "hear no evil, see no evil" monkeys are great for kids of all ages!

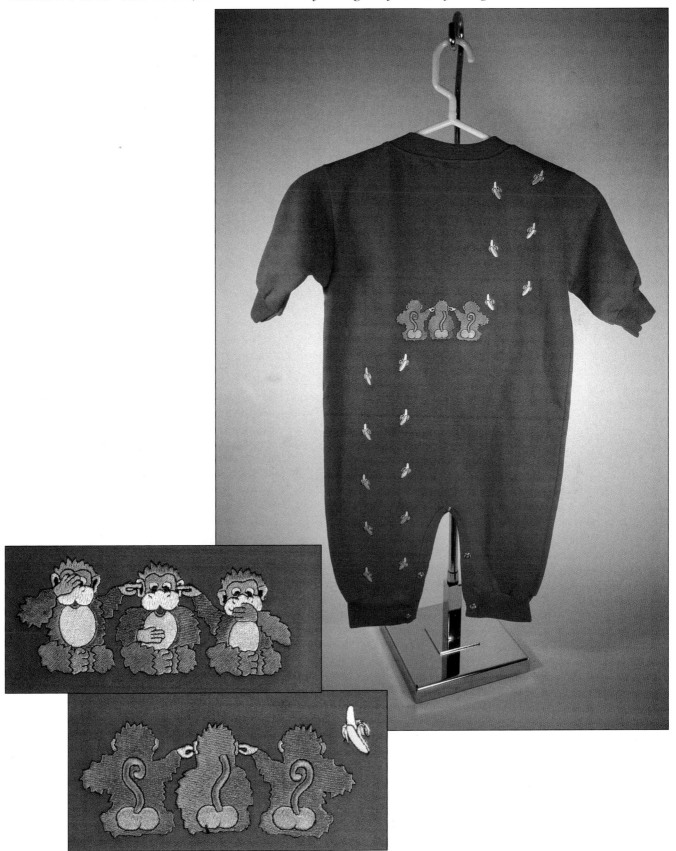

Embroidery by Jeanine, Embroidery Designs by Cactus Punch

One of the best ways to texturize Polarfleece fabric is to use the underlay stitches that lie beneath Cactus Punch's satin stitch designs. The edge of a garment, near the closure, is yet another space where embroidery can be stitched.

Carol Bell Digitized Appliqué

Carol Bell, a Brother International Educator, specializes in appliqué. She digitizes designs using the Brother PE-Design software. Here's a collection of her beautiful appliqués stitched to perfection using the Brother method of appliqué.

Carol digitized the veins of the Ultrasuede leaves with running stitches and the leaf-stems with satin stitches. Since Ultrasuede fabric does not ravel, it was not necessary to completely satin stitch the material in place. The simple running stitch veins hold down the leaf to allow the design to appear multi-dimensional.

Carol digitized the Christmas tree appliqué and then stitched by hand a purchased string of decorative Christmas lights and a star button onto the embroidered fabric, This design fits perfectly into the Brother extra-large hoop.

From birthdays to holidays, appliqué can be used all year round!

Photographs from Viking Sewing Machines

Kids, embroidery and sewing go perfect together! If the design is large, use a larger hoop to stitch the motif. If the design is small, combine several designs and still use a larger hoop. For best results when stitching large designs, embroider the fabric and then sew the garment pieces together.

Embroidered and Sewn by Nicky Bookout; Embroidery Designs by Bubbles Menagerie

A birthday banner, with coordinating streamers, is a great way to celebrate someone's special day. The project was embroidered in one hooping with the aid of the Giant Hoop-It-All frame hoop and the design layout capabilities of the Buzz Tools software.

Photograph and Design from Baby Lock USA

The placement of designs can be just about anywhere. Here's an idea for a non-traditional placement—at the lower edge of the shirt and at the jacket opening. A simple, yet elegant placement of a design can yield couture results.

Embroidered by Nancy Cornwell,
Embroidery Design by Cactus Punch

Nancy Cornwell shows us that combining border print fabric with embroidery not only adds interest to the fabric but is easy to stitch. Using her embroidery design disk from Cactus Punch, Nancy added a flock of flying geese to the sky near the shoulder for subtle interest to the fabric. More embroidery techniques can be found in her Polarfleece book series from Krause Publications.

Embroidered by Elna Educator, Geri Frasier; Embroidery Designs from Elna

Here's a geometric fun wall hanging that is an underwater sea adventure in embroidery. Stitch fish and sea greenery onto fabric and then add a layer of netting with more embroidery.

Embroidered by Linda Crone; Embroidery Designs by Cactus Punch

Linda Crone, author of Fabric Landscapes by Machine, *has a lot of fun making mini embroidered landscapes into greeting cards especially with her design disk from Cactus Punch. The size of the tri-fold greeting card is 6" x 8" with a window opening of 4" x 6"—perfect for just about any embroidery design or landscape. Cards are available from Linda Crone Creations.*

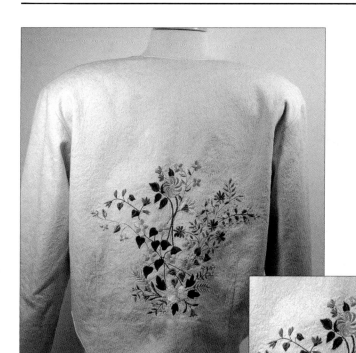

Sewn and Embroidered by Pauline Richards; Embroidery Designs by Viking Sewing Machines

The backside of jackets can provide a wonderful canvas for the combining and arranging of multiple embroidery designs. Pauline Richards combined several Viking embroidery designs to create this beautiful bouquet of flowers. This bouquet would not be possible if it weren't for the large area available on the back of this jacket.

Embroidery and Design By Dakota Collectibles

Stitching designs on black fabric can be dramatic when using all one color of a high-sheen rayon embroidery thread. The thread accentuates the layers and texture of the digitizing. Notice that some areas of the design have an open stitch pattern to allow the base fabric to show through the stitches.

Embroidery and Design from Janome of America

Decorate a purchased jumper with a bouquet of embroidered heart balloons. Perfect for use with embroidery foam, this little girl's jumper is simple to embellish with neon-colored polyester threads.

Embroidered and Sewn by Pauline Richards; Embroidery Designs by Cactus Punch

Embroidered and Sewn by Jeanine; Embroidery Design by Viking Sewing Machines

Making embroidered fabric is simple with a little bit of planning. The secret is to only embroider the area of fabric you'll need for the project. The collar of the pink jacket is embroidered with a Viking all-over connecting design and a portion of the teal jacket is embroidered with Pauline Richard's design disk from Cactus Punch. Both jackets feature embroidered fabric that was stitched prior to the construction of the jacket.

Embroidered and Sewn by Jeanine; Embroidery Design by Cactus Punch

Use the overall measurements of the Polar Pillow project, found on page 81, to make this fun, pieced travel pillow. Stitch up the pillow with decorative quilt making fabric and embroider the area surrounding the button or snap.

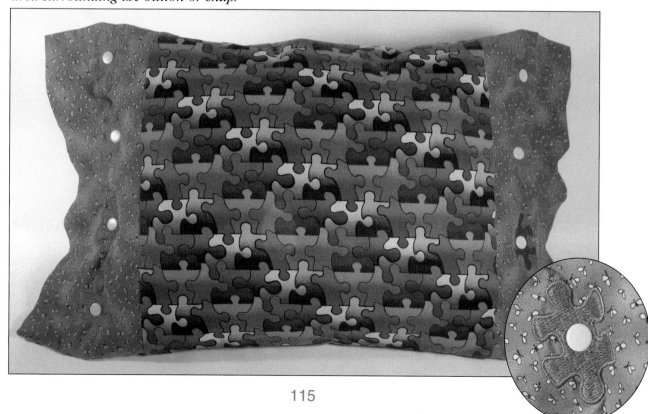

Photograph from Viking Sewing Machines

This elegant garden table setting is beautifully embroidered with the precise arrangement of floral motifs...this picture says a thousand words...

absolutely stunning!

Photograph from Viking Sewing Machines

From blankets to bed pillows to even outerwear, embroidery for your furry friends can be a fun way to show off your design collection. It's also a great way to utilize fabric sections used for the test-stitching of designs. Choose a commonly embroidered fabric for testing and when there is no room left for embroidery, sew up an outfit for your favorite pooch!

Embroidered by Elna Educator, Geri Frasier; Embroidery Designs from Elna

This velvet Christmas stocking has a black organza top header that has been carefully embroidered with gold metallic thread and decorated with a fabric bow and ribbon.

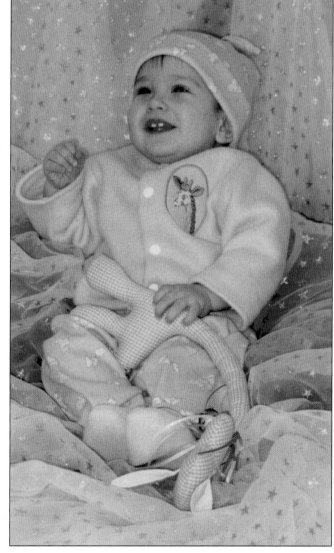

Photograph and Layette Pattern from Sew Baby

Sewing for babies is fun especially when personalized with a bit of embroidery. When considering embroidery in small little areas of clothing, it's helpful to either sew the ensemble from a pattern or open up the seams surrounding the area to be embroidered.

117

Embroidered and Sewn by Nicky Bookout, Embroidery Designs by Bubbles Menagerie

Here's a great idea for a teacher. This pillow project was embroidered with the aid of the time saving Giant Hoop-It-All frame hoop and the design layout capabilities of the Buzz Tools software.

Embroidered by Lindee Goodall; Embroidery Designs and Alphabet from Cactus Punch

Every woman needs an apron like this! Test your lettering skills with this great project idea from Lindee Goodall.

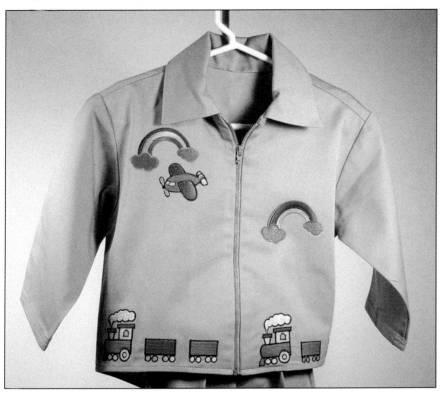

Embroidery and Designs from Elna USA

Decorate clothes for boys with trains, planes and colorful rainbows.

Embroidery and Designs from Dakota Collectibles

The front shoulder area of this denim vest made the perfect canvas for a barnyard scene.

Embroidery and Designs from Dakota Collectibles

Create a garden vest and matching gloves all from one design pack. Separate the designs with bias binding strips sewn to the vest and be sure to decorate the front as well as the back of the vest for visual interest as you're coming and going!

Embroidered and Sewn by Pauline Richards; Embroidery Designs by Cactus Punch

Pauline Richard's geometric designs from Cactus Punch adds even more elegance to this lovely tailored silk suit jacket. For best results, embroider the fabric first before constructing the jacket from a pattern.

Embroidery and Pattern by Sew Baby

A reversible baby bunting made from Polarfleece and interlock knit fabric just wouldn't be the same without a hint of fabric coordinating embroidery.

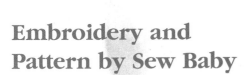

Embroidery and Design by Janome of America

Embroider and sew a creative backpack for kids. Or, purchase a plain flap backpack and embroider it with a decorative design. The pictured design is licensed and should be stitched for personal use only.

Embroidered and Sewn by Lindee Goodall; Embroidery Designs by Cactus Punch

Here's a fun way to tastefully experiment with an entire disk of embroidery designs. Create a Halloween sampler on the front and back of a black vest. Use orange rickrack around the edges when sewing the vest from a pattern.

Back of vest.

122

Embroidery and Design by Janome of America

Embroidery on darker fabrics can effectively show off a light-colored design. Purchased shirts can be one of the easiest ways to show off your embroidery designs. The pictured design is licensed and should be stitched for personal use only.

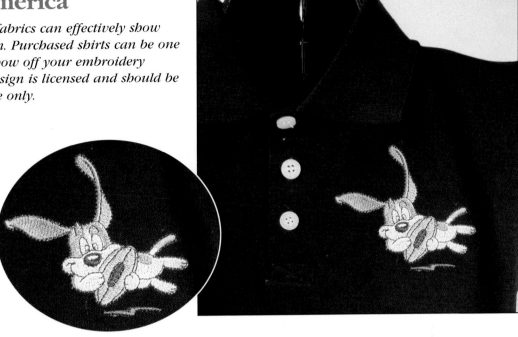

Embroidery by Vicki Madigan, a Brother International Education Consultant; Embroidery design by Brother International

Embroidery on purchased jeans is simple when the inner or outer seam of the leg is opened up to accommodate the hoop. Follow the instructions of Project #20 on page 96 to embroider the bottom of the jeans. Machine stitch a large rickrack braiding around the waist for added embellishment.

Embroidery and Designs from Dakota Collectibles

Here's a great idea for a pocket—the school supplies design is called a "pocket topper". There are many companies that offer these types of embroidery designs. If you are using a purchased garment with a pocket, carefully remove the pocket before the embroidery process. If you are sewing the item from a pattern, be sure to embroider the pocket and pocket topper before constructing the garment.

Embroidery and Design by Janome of America

Stitch a random placement of flowers on a 12" square of fabric. Add a decorative border and sew the pieces of fabric pieces into a pillow. The flowers chosen match the fabric border. Also, experiment with digitizing designs to match the fabric.

Appendix I

Troubleshooting

This section will help provide answers to the most common embroidery problems. If you are still having difficulty with your machine after trying some of these problem-solving tips, consult the dealership where your machine warranty is being honored.

> *Nicky Bookout, freelance instructor and designer for Bubbles Menagerie, says: "We get the most creative when we have to 'fix' our mistakes!"*

Thread

Not every thread is going to stitch perfectly in your machine. If you have problems, consider the direction in which the thread is being unwound off the spool. Specialty threads should be unwound off the spool naturally and into the thread path—vertically on the machine and horizontally on a thread stand behind or next to the machine. Some threads behave better when unwound off the front of the spool and others off the back of the spool. If you are having problems with certain threads, change the direction the spool is being unwound can make a big difference. Also, to save on lint build up in your upper tension, clip threads by the spool when changing colors. Pull the excess thread through the needle and discard.

Looping of Stitches

Are you using polyester thread? It may be necessary to tighten the upper tension to prevent looping with polyester thread.

Is there a burr on the needle? If you run your finger over the end of the needle and feel a bump, a burr may have formed from the result of the needle penetrating the fabric and stabilizer. Change the needle.

Is the needle sticky from adhesive stabilizer? Sometimes needles become sticky from adhesive stabilizers. A quick fix would be to clean the needle with a 'goo' remover. Be sure to wipe the remover off the needle to eliminate the possibility of fabric staining. Change needles often or slow down the stitching speed.

Has your machine been in for service lately? Have your machine serviced to clean the lint from the tension disks for a smooth running machine.

Is your machine threaded correctly? Check the path of the thread through the top tension area. It may be necessary to re-thread the machine. Be sure the bobbin thread is secure in the machine; it may be necessary to wind another bobbin. Be sure to raise the presser foot before threading the machine to open up the tension area to accept the thread. Lower the presser foot to thread the needle. Do not pull on the thread once the pressure foot is lowered.

Thread Breakage

Are the fabric and stabilizer in the hoop correctly? Hoop the fabric and stabilizer so they are taut. Use a spray adhesive to temporarily secure the fabric and stabilizer together before the hooping process to prevent the shifting of the two pieces of material.

Is the thread hooked on something in its path to the needle? Be sure the thread is not obstructed anywhere from the spool to the needle.

Is the design too dense? Choose a lighter-weight thread, a cut-away stabilizer or another design.

Is the thread twisting as it enters the tension disks? Be sure the thread is unwinding from the spool or cone properly. Sometimes it is necessary to change the direction the thread is unwinding from the spool or cone in order for the thread to travel straight into the tension area of the machine. Use a cone holder or a thread stand, if necessary.

Is the thread a metallic or specialty thread? Use a metallic needle with a larger eye for metallic or specialty threads. If the metallic or specialty thread is being used with a dense design, consider switching to another thread for better results. Use specialty threads on a vertical spool holder in the machine.

Is the needle new? If the answer is no, change the needle. If the answer is yes, then the eye of the needle may have a sharp edge or the eye of the needle is too small. Replace the needle.

Is the needle the correct type or size for the fabric, thread and stabilizer? Change to another needle type or size.

Is your machine stitching at high speed? Slow down the machine stitching for more control.

Is the tension adjusted correctly? Loosen the upper tension.

Is the bobbin wound correctly and through the bobbin tension area? Be sure the bobbin is wound at a reduced speed. When winding a bobbin at full speed the thread packs into the bobbin very tightly and can cause thread breaks. Be sure the bobbin is in the bobbin tension area on the machine or in the bobbin case.

Metallic Thread Difficulties

Is the correct needle being used? Be sure to use a needle manufactured for use with metallic thread.

Is your machine stitching at high speed? Slow down the machine when stitching with metallic threads to keep the tension constant.

Is the thread shredding? When a metallic thread is used in a dense design, the rubbing of the thread against one another tends to break down the metallic wrapping of the fiber. Switch to a higher quality thread, another design or stitch the thread alone in a single-color design.

Is the needle new? The needle eye may have a burr. Discard the needle and switch to a new one.

Is the thread kinking as it unwinds from the spool? Metallic threads tend to run smoother when being unwound from the spool vertically in the machine and horizontally from a separate thread stand to prevent kinking.

Birdsnest on the Backside of the Fabric

Is the presser foot lever in the correct position? The pressure foot can cause a birdsnest if it is too high or too low to the fabric. Be sure to check to see if your machine has an automatic or manual presser foot resting position.

Is the thread tension correct? The upper thread tension may be too low. Increase the upper thread tension.

Is the machine threaded correctly? Make sure the decorative thread is secure in the upper tension. It is best to thread the machine while the pressure foot is up to allow the thread to be placed securely in the tension area.

Bobbin Thread is Coming to the Top of the Design

Is the bobbin wound correctly? Try using another threaded bobbin and wind the bobbin at a reduced speed.

Is the correct weight of thread being used in the bobbin? Use a 60-weight or higher bobbin thread.

Is there lint in the area surrounding the bobbin? Clean the area surrounding the bobbin to remove any lint build-up especially when using cotton or cotton blend bobbin thread, which tends to leave more of a lint build-up.

Is the tension adjusted correctly? Loosen the upper tension, if necessary.

Is the correct needle being used for the fabric and stabilizer? Change the needle, if necessary.

Fabric Showing Through the Threads

Is a standard 40-weight thread being used? Use a 30-weight thread for better coverage. Or, slightly reduce the size of the design to change the density for better coverage.

Is a topping being used? Use a water-soluble topping to hold down the nap of the fabric during the embroidery process. A permanent vinyl, in the color of the thread, can prevent the fabric from showing through, too.

Scratchy Threads on the Backside of the Design

Sometimes the scratchy backsides of embroidery designs can be caused by the texture of stitched threads. This can be unbearable to wear next to the skin. Try some of these steps to eliminate the scratchy texture of an embroidered design:

Fuse a layer of tricot interfacing slightly larger than the design to the backside of the fabric.

Slide a layer of a soft, lightweight cut-away stabilizer under the hoop just prior to the outline stitch. Trim any excess stabilizer to 1/4" from the outline stitch.

Use cotton embroidery thread (in the bobbin, too). This type of thread can feel softer next to the skin.

Loosen your upper thread tension.

If your design does not have an outline stitch and you want to use a soft, lightweight cut-away stabilizer on the backside of the design, remove the hoop from the machine with the fabric still in the hoop. Use a

spray adhesive to adhere a piece of cut-away stabilizer to the backside of the hooped fabric. Using a sewing machine, stitch close to the outer edge of the design using an invisible thread or a color that coordinates with the fabric. Trim away the stabilizer close to the stitching.

Choose a design with longer stitches such as satin or fill-in stitches to allow more bobbin thread to be exposed on backside of the embroidery design. Short, compact stitches can be scratchy especially with more color changes.

Tie-off threads can cause a design to be itchy, too. Choose designs with minimal color changes.

> June Mellinger, director of education with Brother International says, "If you're getting a poor quality stitch, re-thread both the needle thread and the bobbin thread. If the stitch is still not precise, replace the needle and determine if a different size needle is needed. Still not right? Replace or change the thread and see if it makes a difference. If you're using a pre-wound bobbin, it could be the culprit."

Needle Problems

With so many needle sizes to choose from, it's sometimes hard to determine which needle to use for what fabric. This is why the test-stitch process is so important. It's better to find out what's wrong on a test sample than to experience problems on the real project. Most of the time when there are problems with the embroidery process, the needle is usually the guilty party. Sometimes it is just a matter of changing the needle to fix the problem.

Needle Breakage

Is the thread hooked on something in its path to the needle? Be sure the thread is not obstructed anywhere from the spool to the needle.

Is the design too dense? Choose a lighter-weight thread or another design.

Is the needle the correct type or size for the fabric, thread and stabilizer? Change to another needle type or size.

Sticky Needle

Has the needle become sticky with adhesive? Remove the needle from the machine and clean it with an adhesive cleaning agent. Be sure to clean the needle thoroughly as to not leave any residue that may transfer to the fabric.

Are the designs being stitched at full speed? Reduce the speed of the stitching to prevent the needle from heating up during the embroidery process.

Needle Holes in Fabric

Is the correct needle size being used for the fabric? Change the needle to a smaller size.

Is a heavyweight thread being used for stitching? Use a lighter-weight thread for the embroidery process.

Stabilizer Problems

Using the proper stabilizer for a project can make the difference in the end result. There are so many different brands of stabilizers. It may just be a matter of switching brands to achieve successful results. Upon examination of a test-stitched design, it is fairly simple to determine whether or not the correct stabilizer was used.

Stabilizer Being Stitched Away

Is a tear-away being used for a dense design? Switch to a cut-away stabilizer. The needle is literally cutting away the stabilizer from the design, which is leaving your fabric and design open for distortion problems.

Is your fabric a knit? Switch to a cut-away stabilizer. Knit fabric can stretch during the embroidery process if not properly stabilized causing the stabilizer to be stitched away from the design.

Adhesive Stabilizer Stuck to Back of Hoop

Has an adhesive stabilizer been on the back of the hoop for a long time? Adhesive stabilizers can be a form of contact adhesive. The longer it remains the stickier it becomes. Therefore, remove the adhesive stabilizer immediately after the embroidery process. Start with a fresh piece of stabilizer with every new design.

Have you tried a non-alcohol cleaner to remove the sticky substance? Use a non-alcohol-based solvent to clean the surface. Some spray adhesives are removable with soap and water. Others need something more powerful.

Hooping Problems

A hoop holds the fabric and the stabilizer taut during the embroidery process. Should the correct fabric and stabilizer be used, but the hooping method is incorrect, the project could still have many problems.

Hoop Burn or Marks on Fabric

Is velvet, velour or polarfleece hooped? Use hoopless embroidery method (page 47).

Is silk or linen hooped? Sandwich the fabric between a topping and a backing.

Is the embroidery complete? Steam the fabric on the top of the fabric (do not press). Use your hand or a very soft brush to 'fluff up' the fabric.

Is the fabric washable? Sometimes washing the fabric will remove the mark or burn.

> *Lindee says, "Leaving garments hooped longer than necessary before or after stitching increases the chance of hoop marks."*

Hoop Movement Problems

Is the hoop free of obstruction? Be sure to leave adequate space around your machine for embroidery. The area in which you embroider should be free of articles that would inhibit the free-motion of the embroidery machine arm that moves the hoop during the embroidery process. When using overly large hoops it is best to allow plenty of room for the machine to move the hoop to stitch the design.

Are the feed teeth down? Be sure the feed teeth on the bed of the machine are recessed into the machine to allow the hoop to freely pass over the bed of the machine.

Has a birdsnest formed on the backside of the hoop at the throat plate? Remove the hoop from the machine and carefully clip any threads connecting the hoop to the machine. Gently remove any threads imbedded in the throat plate and in the bobbin housing. Trim away any threads on the backside of the hoop and remove the stitches that formed the birdsnest. If your pressure foot is raised manually, be sure it is in the correct position. Tighten the upper tension on the machine.

Fabric Problems

With the infinite number of fabrics available, it takes a bit of trial and error to achieve the right combination of embroidery products to stitch a design correctly.

The Fabric is Puckering Around the Design

Are your fabric and stabilizer hooped taut? Re-hoop the fabric correctly and re-test the design. Consider using a spray adhesive to temporarily stick the fabric and the stabilizer together during the hooping process to prevent puckering.

Is your fabric too light for the design? Choose an open, airy design on the fabric with a lightweight stabilizer.

Is the fabric a knit? Interface the fabric before the hooping process.

Is the correct stabilizer being used? If the answer is yes, then slide another piece of the same stabilizer between the hooped fabric and the bed of the machine. The extra stabilizer will help hold the design better.

Is the stabilizer a tear-away? The design may stitch better with a cut-away stabilizer. If the design is dense, the needle penetrations may be cutting away the tear-away stabilizer and creating an unstable design. Switch to a cut-away stabilizer. It may be necessary to switch to another design for the fabric.

Sara Meyer-Snuggerud, director of marketing for OESD, says, "There are several problems that can cause puckering of a design or fabric—the most common is a problem with the hooping process. The first thing to remember is that you should never stretch your fabric when placing it in the hoop. The fabric will remain stretched and puckered after the embroidery process. Your best insurance for hooping and puckering difficulties is to use a temporary spray adhesive. Spray the appropriate stabilizer with spray adhesive. With the sticky side up, lay the sprayed stabilizer on a flat surface. Lay the fabric to be hooped over the stabilizer making sure the fabric is not stretched—you want the fabric to be relaxed and smooth on the stabilizer. Once you have the fabric stabilized, you can hoop it without fear of stretching."

Project Caught on the Underside of the Hoop or the Topside of the Stitching

It's important to make sure the surrounding fabric of a garment is away from the area on top or under the hoop during the stitching process. There is potential for the surrounding fabric or garment to get caught in the stitching if not cleared from the movement of the needle. Should the garment or fabric get caught in the stitches, stop the machine and remove the hoop from the machine. If possible, gently remove the stitches to free the fabric. If this is not possible, the project will be damaged. Restart the embroidery process with a new garment or piece of fabric.

Design Problems

Professionally digitized designs are rarely the cause of design problems. In most cases, the fabric and stabilizer were not hooped properly or the incorrect embroidery products were used. This is why test stitching is so vitally important to the success of any project. Test the design's compatibility with the fabric and embroidery products to determine if there is a problem before stitching on the actual project.

Designs Look Flat

Has the design been steam pressed? If the fabric can be ironed, steam press the design on the backside of the fabric with a press cloth and a well padded ironing board.

Where was the design digitized? Some designs

are digitized with a flat appearance, while others are digitized with added stitches to add dimension. Choose designs according to your personal preference knowing that some designs are produced without dimension.

Is the correct stabilizer being used for the fabric? Choose a stabilizer with more holding power for the design. If the design is dense with a lot of stitches, use a cut-away stabilizer.

Lindee says: "Machine tensions can cause a flat look to designs. If the tensions are too tight, they can pull the stitches into the fabric. The only way to correct this is to adjust the tensions and stitch again."

Outline of Design is not Accurate

Is the fabric stabilized correctly? With designs containing outlines, the fabric must be stabilized correctly. Use the hoopless embroidery method found on page 47 or use a spray adhesive to temporarily hold the fabric to the stabilizer during the hooping process.

Lindee says: "Another reason could be tight thread tensions pulling the stitching shorter in the fill and satin areas of the design—loosen your tension."

Has the design just been purchased over the Internet or recently converted to your embroidery machine format? The design may have been damaged during the transfer process. Retry the transfer process or try to get the design in the original format from the source.

Patricia D.A. "Patty" Reinert, embroidery technician/coordinator for Dakota Collectibles, says, "Different fabrics, backings and hooping techniques govern how well a design will stitch. On rare occasions, you may experience difficulty in getting the detail lines to outline properly. Consider using your editing capabilities in your computer software program to move the fill stitches and/or the detail lines. Learning this editing technique is perhaps the greatest favor you can do for yourself. With just a little practice, you can become quite proficient at this procedure. Save your edited version on a disk or your computer. Never copy over the original data, take your time and experiment to adjust the design to fit your specific embroidery application."

Skipped Stiches or Open Space

Are there stitches in the design that did not embroider correctly? If going over the area on the embroidery machine is not an option, use the sewing capabilities of your machine, or a sewing machine to stitch over the design area. Keep the fabric in the hoop, drop the machine's feed dogs, set the machine to straight stitch and fill in the area of the design using sewing machine stitches.

Are there open spaces in the design with the fabric showing through? Use the editing capabilities of your embroidery machine or computer software to reduce the size of the design to compensate for the open spaces. Stitching with a thicker 30-weight thread can also be used to compensate for this problem.

Appendix II

Test Stitch Evaluation Sheet

Design/Pack: _____Company: _____

List thread(s):

Brand	Fiber	Weight	Color	Number

List stabilizer(s):

Brand	Style	Comments

Needle size: _____ Brand: _____ Style: _____

Hoop size: _____

Fabric: _____

Was a template included with the purchase of the design?

Did you make your own template and is it included in this notebook?

Overall Comments:

_____

_____

Glossary of Terms

Accessory: An embroidery notion, tool or apparatus that can be of assistance during the embroidery process.

Acrylic thread: A strong, synthetic fiber that has medium sheen and is bleach resistant.

Adhesive: The sticky residue found on some stabilizers or added to stabilizers from a spray can. It can be used to secure items without hooping or to adhere layers together temporarily.

All-over design: A design that is stitched in sections over an entire area to form a continuous pattern.

Appliqué: An embroidery technique that involves the applying of one fabric to the surface of another. The fabric is held down with embroidery stitches and can be used to replace a large area of fill stitches.

Artwork: Original clipart or hand drawings that can be used to form digitized designs.

Backing: A stabilizer that is used on the back of fabric during the embroidery process. (see also stabilizer)

Baste: Placing large running stitches by machine or by hand onto fabric to temporarily hold layers together.

Birdsnest: A problem that consists of a collection of threads jammed together on the backside of a design between the fabric and the throat plate of the machine. A bird's-nest can be caused by incorrect machine tension or by the improper hooping of the embroidery project.

Bobbin: A double-ended, compressed spool that holds the bobbin thread and fits into the embroidery machine under or near the embroidery foot. The bobbin thread forms the stitches on the underside of the fabric.

Card: A small, flat device that is programmed with decorative designs. The card fits directly into an embroidery machine and is read by the machine's computer.

Card read/writer box: The piece of hardware that aids in the transfer of designs between the computer and the embroidery machine.

Chain stitch: An embroidery decorative stitch that looks like a chain link which can add texture to a stitched design.

Chenille: A loop-type stitch most commonly found on school letter jackets. It's a form of raised embroidery where the stitch is on the top-side of the fabric and made of heavy yarns like wool, cotton or acrylic. A special machine is used to form this stitch.

Colorfast: A thread's ability to retain its color during normal wear and laundering.

Colorize: The method of choosing colors of thread for embroidery designs; choosing thread colors other than what the manufacturer suggests.

Computerized embroidery: The ability to stitch decorative designs on a computerized embroidery machine. Also known as "automatic embroidery".

Cone: A large, angled cylinder that thread is wound onto for use in the commercial embroidery industry.

Copyright: A legal term that refers to the ownership of original designs or artwork. The copyright law protects the designer or artist from unauthorized use of their designs.

Core: The main strand used to form metallic thread fibers.

Cotton thread: A natural fiber thread that has a low sheen and comes in the largest array of sizes.

Cross-over embroidery: The embroidery technique involving another craft form (stencils, paints, ribbon embroidery, rubber stamps) with the stitching of decorative designs.

Cross-stitch: A stitch that forms an "x" on fabric. The look of hand cross-stitch embroidery can be achieved on an embroidery machine with the aid of properly digitized designs or software.

Cupping: The curling of dense designs on fabric that are improperly stabilized.

Curved scissors: Scissors that are curved upward at the tip to enable a clean, close cut of embroidery threads.

Custom designs: Designs digitized by a professional company with original artwork. Custom designs are most commonly made for companies or individuals that want a design digitized for a specific use.

Customizing: The changing of a design to meet personal specifications. Enlarging, reducing, rotating, colorizing and adding letters to a design are forms of customizing.

Cut-away: A stabilizer that is cut-away from the fabric after the embroidery process.

Cutwork: An embroidery technique in which the base material is cut-away to reveal the stabilizer. After the embroidery cutwork process, the stabilizer is removed to form smoothly stitched holes in the design.

Decorative fill: Large areas of stitches that have a textured stitch pattern. (see Fill stitches.)

Density: The number of stitches that form a design. A high-density design has a high stitch count. Design: A decorative motif that is stitched using an embroidery machine.

Design transfer: The ability to move designs to and from the computer and embroidery machine via a cable, read/writer box, computer software or the Internet.

Digitizing: The process of adding stitches to a piece of artwork to form a computer-generated embroidery design.

Dimensional embroidery: Designs that are stitched onto a sheer fabric and then cut close to the outside edge of the stitching. The designs are then stitched onto another material that results in a raised dimensional appliqué.

Disk: A computer accessory that stores designs and software to be loaded directly into your computer or embroidery machine.

Downloading: The transfer of designs from the Internet to the computer, from the computer to the read/writer box, from the read/writer box to the embroidery machine or from the computer to the embroidery machine.

Editing: Using a computer software program or the screen of an embroidery machine to change stitch-based designs.

Elasticity: The ability of a thread to stretch without breaking and then return to its original shape during the embroidery process.

Embroidery: The stitching of decorative designs onto fabric using an embroidery machine.

Fiber: A natural or synthetic strand of material that can be made into thread or fabric.

File extensions/formats: The last three characters after the period in a computer file name. These characters designate which software program can read the file.

Fill stitch: Elongated stitches that are formed closely together to cover a large area of one color in a design. The stitches can be flat or form a textured design pattern. (see also Decorative fill.)

Finishing: The final stage of the embroidery process where threads are trimmed, stabilizer is removed and the fabric and design are pressed or steamed. (see also Trimming)

Flagging: The wavy movement of the hooped fabric during the embroidery process as the result of loosely hooped goods. Flagging can cause a bird's-nest, puckering and a poorly stitched design.

Foam: A pliable, compressible material used as a topping under specially digitized satin stitches to form a raised embroidery effect.

Foam raised embroidery: Foam raised embroidery is a technique in which embroidery foam is used as a topping to lift the decorative threads off the base fabric. The threads are stitched over the foam to offer visual interest to the design. The embroidery needle self-cuts the foam for a clean finish.

Foil: A narrow, flat metal film used alone or formed around a core fiber to create a specialty thread such as holographic or glitter threads.

Fringing: An embroidery technique that uses unusually long digitized stitches formed closely together and secured on one end by an area of fill stitches. The bobbin threads of the long stitches are clipped allowing the long stitches to be pulled to the surface forming securely looped threads.

Guide stitches: Digitized stitches that form an outline for the placement of appliqué patterns or fabric. Sometimes used in multiple hoop designs to align the placement of the next motif.

Hardware: Pieces of equipment that are used for embroidery such as a computer, embroidery machine, scanner, printer or card read/writer box.

Hoop (Noun): A two-piece device that attaches to the embroidery machine's arm to hold the fabric and stabilizer during the embroidery process.

Hoop (Verb): The action of holding the fabric and stabilizer taut during the embroidery process.

Hoop burn: The temporary or permanent mark that remains on the fabric after the hoop has been removed. Visual evidence that the fabric was hooped with the shape of the hoop imbedded into the fabric.

Hooping aid: Any device that assists with the hooping process; from products which help align designs in a hoop to hooping boards that assist with placement of designs.

Hoopless embroidery: An embroidery technique where the stabilizer and fabric are not hooped. An adhesive stabilizer, which is secured to the back of the hoop, holds the fabric during the embroidery process.

Interfacing: A material that is fused to the back of fabric in an effort to stabilize the fabric before the hooping process. Interfacings are mostly used on knit fabrics.

Internet: A worldwide network of companies, individuals and electronic mailboxes accessible with a computer and a connecting service. Embroidery designs, companies and products are available for downloading, viewing or purchasing.

Jump stitch: A long stitch that skips over fabric after one design finishes and the next begins.

Lacework: An embroidery technique that involves the stitching of threads onto a water-soluble base stabilizer or sheer fabric to make a lace appliqué.

Lettering: The stitching of alphabetic characters onto a base material that can be mixed with an embroidery design or stitched alone.

Lock stitch: The small compact stitches used at the end of each design, change in stitch pattern or color change to tie-off the thread and to prevent the design from becoming unstitched.

Logo: A design created especially for a name, trademark or symbol. The owner of the logo holds the copyright.

Long stitches: Stitches that are long such as satin stitches and running stitches.

Looping: A problem with threads that are raised unevenly on the surface of a stitched design. Usually caused by poor upper tension, a burr on the tip of the needle or by a sticky needle.

Marking: Making temporary hand-drawn spots on fabric to denote important placement, such as the hoop cross hatch and a design start point.

Memory: The part of the embroidery machine, card, disk or computer that saves and remembers changes or new designs, lettering or stitching sequences for future use. The memory is only limited to the capacity of the machine, card, disk or computer.

Metallic thread: Thread made from metal material that is wrapped around core material and is commonly used to add sparkle to a design.

Monogram: The embroidery technique of using of one or more letters as the initials of a name. Most commonly used on towels, bed linens and clothing for identification purposes.

Motif: A stitched embroidery design.

Nap: The directional texture of the fabric pile commonly found on fabrics with long raised fibers, such as Polarfleece, velour or velvet.

Needle: The straight metal device that is inserted into the embroidery machine to hold the thread and help form an embroidery stitch. Needles are available in different sizes and styles depending on the weight of the thread and fabric to be embroidered.

On-screen editing: The ability to edit designs on the touch screen of an embroidery machine.

Outline stitch: A running and finishing stitch that surrounds the outside of a design.

Patch: An embroidery design that is stitched onto a base material for placement onto another project or fabric. An outer flange of material is kept for securing onto another fabric.

Pilot Long, raised fibers that protrude from the base of the material. Fabrics with a pile should be used with a topping to hold down the fibers and keep the embroidery stitches from sinking into the fabric.

Placement: The pre-determined location of embroidery designs that are usually marked on the fabric with a temporary marker. (see also Marking)

Polyester thread: A strong, durable thread that has some elasticity and is bleach resistant.

Pre-wound bobbin: Bobbin thread pre-wound in a factory with or without generic sized cardboard or plastic disposable sides. Pre-wound bobbins are most commonly used in commercial embroidery machines.

Puckering: The wavy ridges formed around an embroidery design that could be caused by too dense of a design for the fabric, loose hooping of the fabric and stabilizer, incorrect backing material to support the design, a dull needle or incorrect tension.

Rayon thread: A natural, high-sheen fiber that is one of the most popular decorative threads for embroidery. It is used for specialty projects, is smooth running and requires special laundry techniques.

Registration: The alignment of the stitches that correctly form the embroidery design.

Reverse applique: An embroidery technique in which a piece of decorative fabric is stitched on the backside of the base material. The base material is then cut-away between areas of stitching to reveal the decorative fabric—similar to cutwork and the opposite of appliqué.

Running stitch: A continuous line of single stitches, between two points, commonly used in fill, underlay, outline and quilt stitches.

Satin stitch: Zigzag stitches that are digitized close together to form a column. Satin stitches can be stitched in all directions.

Scaling/sizing: The ability to

change the size of a design.

Scanning: The method of copying an original piece of artwork directly to the computer via a piece of hardware called a "scanner".

Sewability: The determination of whether a thread can perform under normal embroidery stitching.

Sheen: The shine of a thread.

Short stitches: Small stitches that cover little areas of a design.

Shrinkage: The amount a thread or design shrinks under normal washing conditions. A quality thread product shrinks minimally, if at all.

Software: Items used in the embroidery process such as computer programs, computer disks and cards.

Soldering iron/hot knife: A hot device that is used to melt or trim sheer nylon fabric close to the threads of the design; most commonly used for dimensional embroidery.

Specialty threads: Threads that are used to add sparkle and glitter effects to embroidery designs. From holographic to foil threads, specialty threads usually require a special needle and should be unwound from a vertical spool holder in the machine or a horizontal spool holder behind or beside the machine.

Spool: A small cylinder onto which thread is wound.

Spray adhesive: Liquid adhesive applied to fabric or stabilizer from an aerosol can.

Stabilizer: A material used to protect and prevent distortion of the fabric during the embroidery process. Stabilizers are available in many weights, sizes and styles. (See Backing and Topping.)

Step stitch: The stitches between alphabetic letters or small areas of a design in which starting and stopping of a design would be inefficient.

Stitch count: The number of stitches in a design.

Stitch direction: The direction in which stitches are sewn within an embroidery design. A change in a stitch direction adds depth and texture to a design.

Stitch gap: The area(s) of a design where stitches should have been sewn. A stitch gap can be caused by poor registration, embroidery arm interference or improperly hooped fabric and stabilizer.

Stitch-out: A design that has been embroidered onto a base material as a test or a sample.

Stock designs: Designs that are digitized and available for sale.

Surge protector: An outlet to plug embroidery equipment that protects against damage from surges of electricity during storms or power outages.

Tear-away: A stabilizer that is torn-away from the fabric after the embroidery process.

Templates: Clear, plastic, or paper guides to aid in placement of embroidery designs and are most commonly sold with hoops or embroidery designs.

Tension: The embroidery machine's ability to keep the embroidery thread taut while forming stitches. The machine's top tension and bobbin tension must be in harmony to form the properly balanced stitches for embroidery.

Test-stitch: The process of stitching designs on fabric similar or the same as the fabric of the project. Test-stitching should be completed before the embroidery process to determine if the design is suitable for the fabric and that the correct stabilizer and threads are being utilized.

Thread: A fine strand of natural or synthetic fibers used to form embroidery stitches. Look for threads that are specially made for embroidery and available in various weights, colors and styles.

Thread stand: A pegged shelving unit to hold threads during the embroidery process.

Tonal embroidery: An embroidery technique in which designs are stitched with one color of thread that blends with the base fabric color. Also known as tone-on-tone embroidery.

Topping: A stabilizer that is used on the top of fabric during the embroidery process. (See also Stabilizer.)

Trimming: The clipping of top and bobbin threads during and after the embroidery process.

Troubleshooting: The ability to solve problems that occur during the embroidery process.

Underlay stitches: These important stitches stabilize the design area, secure the base fabric to the stabilizer and hold the design in shape during and after the embroidery process.

Uploading: The transfer of designs from the embroidery machine to the computer, from the embroidery machine to the read/writer box, from the read/writer box to the computer, from the computer to the Internet.

Variegated thread: Thread that has multiple colors throughout the spool. The colors vary continually throughout the spool and are available in a large assortment of multiple color schemes.

Resources

Here's a listing of companies that manufacture or sell embroidery products. As always, look for these and other embroidery-related products at your local retailer where embroidery products are sold. You may also visit my Web site at **www.embroideryresource.com** for a complete listing of these and other sources for computerized machine embroidery products.

Listing of Embroidery Products by Category

Home Embroidery Machines and Hardware

Baby Lock
Bernina
Brother
Elna
Husqvarna/ Viking

Janome
Kenmore
Pfaff
Simplicity
Singer

Thread

A&E (Mettler & Signature)
ARC
Brother International
Coats & Clark
DMC
Fabric Loft (Aurifil)
Ghee's
Gutermann
Herrschners
Hoop-It-All
Husqvarna/ Viking
Janome

Madeira USA
OESD (Isacord, SolarActive & Yenmet)
Robison-Anton
SolarActive
Sulky of America
Superior Threads
Tristan (Aurifil)
Tacony (Finishing Touch)
Uncommon Thread
Web of Threads
YLI

Stabilizers

Emblematic
Hoop-It-All
HTC
Husqvarna/ Viking (America Sews)
OESD

Pellon
Sew Baby!
Sulky
Tacony (Finishing Touch)

Software

Amazing Designs
Baby Lock
Bernina
Brother
Building Blocks
Buzz Tools
Elna
Hobbyware
Husqvarna/ Viking

Janome
Madeira
Melco
Pantograms
Pfaff
OESD
Singer
Stitch Shop

Designs

Baby Lock
Balboa Threadworks
Bernina
Brother
Bubbles Menagerie
Building Blocks
Buzz Tools
Cactus Punch
Criswell Embroidery
Dakota Collectibles
Elna
Embroideryarts
Hobbyware
Husqvarna/ Viking
Janome
KMAC Embroidery
OESD
Pfaff
Martha Pullen
Singer
Sudberry House
Suzanne Hinshaw
Tina's Crosstitch Designs
Vermillion Stitchery

Hooping Aids

ABC Embroidery
Baby Lock
Bernina
Brother
Cactus Punch
Elna
Hoop-It-All
Husqvarna/ Viking
Janome
PD Sixty
Perfect Hooper (The)
Pfaff
Sew Special/Sew Simple Hooper
Singer

Scissors

Gingher
Havel's
Hummingbird House
All sewing machine companies

Needles

Madeira
OESD (Organ)
Schmetz
All sewing machine companies

Thread Stands

Husqvarna/Viking
June Tailor
PD Sixty
ThreadPro

Blank Greeting Cards

Linda Crone Creations
Paper Creations

Miscellaneous

Doumar Products: un-do adhesive remover
Dragon Threads: Fiber Etch fabric remover gel
Ghee's: Sparkle organza, embroidery cards & ideas
Hugo's Amazing Tape
Malden Mills: Polarfleece fabrics
Mary's Productions: Appliqué books, patterns, embroidery disks
Mountainland Manufacturing: Thread Pallette, thread holders
PD Sixty: Machine stand, thread stand, specialty hoops
Peggy's Stitch Eraser
Pres-On: Fabric framing boards
Sew Tote: Sturdy machine totes
The Snap Source: Snaps and attaching tools

Furniture

Baby Lock
Elna
Horn of America

Husqvarna/Viking
SCS USA
Sylvia Design Sewing Furniture

Publications

Arts & Crafts Magazine
Creative Machine Embroidery Magazine
Designs in Machine Embroidery Magazine
Embroidery Enthusiast Magazine

Sew Beautiful Magazine
SewNews Magazine
Threads Magazine
Total Embellishment Newsletter

Mail Order

Clotilde
5T's Embroidery Supply
Nancy's Notions

Sew Baby!
Speed Stitch
Web of Thread

Internet Sites of Interest

www.emblibrary.com
www.embstore.com
www.embroidery.com
www.embroiderydirect.com
www.embroideryonline.com
www.embroideryresource.com
www.embroiderthis.com

www.everythingembroidery.com
www.homeembroiderymall.com
www.sewart.com
www.sewstuff.com
www.schmetzneedles.com
www.threadart.com
www.threadartist.com

Organizations

American Sewing Guild
Embroidery Software Protection Coalition

Home Sewing Association

Embroidery & Sewing Events

www.sewexpo.com
www.sewingevents.com

www.sewingexpo.com

Commercial Supplies & Equipment

ARC—Accessory Resource Corp.
Barudan
Brother Embroidery Systems
Floriani
Great Notions
Hirsch International
Madeira

Melco Embroidery Systems
National Embroidery Supply
Pantograms
Robison-Anton
SWF America
Tajima-West

Commercial Publications & Organizations

Bobbin Magazine
Craft & Needlework Age (CNA)
Embroidery Business News Magazine
Embroidery/Monogram Business Magazine

Embroidery Trade Association
Impressions Magazine
National Network of Embroidery Professionals
Stitches Magazine

Listing of Companies

* Indicates companies that provided embroidery products pictured in this book.

ABC Embroidery Systems *
See your local sewing & embroidery dealer.
Call 1-800-748-9433 for a dealer near you.
www.abcemb.com

Amazing Designs *
See your local sewing & embroidery dealer.
Call 1-888-874-6760 for a dealer near you.
www.amazingdesigns.com

American & Efird (A&E) *
See your local sewing & embroidery dealer.
Call 1-800-847-3235 for a dealer near you.
www.amefird.com

American Sewing Guild
Call 1-713-729-3000
www.asg.org

ARC—Accessory Resource Corp.
Call 1-800-877-4272
www.melco.com/ARC

***Arts & Crafts* Magazine**
Subscription information
Call 1-800-258-0929
www.krause.com

Baby Lock USA *
See your local Baby Lock dealer.
Call 1-800-422-2952 for a dealer near you.
www.babylock.com

Balboa Threadworks
Call 1-800-445-8705
www.balboastitch.com
www.balboathreadworks. com

Barudan
Call 1-800-627-4776
www.barudan.com

Bernina of America
See your local Bernina dealer.
Call 1-800-405-2739 for a dealer near you.
www.berninausa.com

***Bobbin* Magazine**
Subscription information
Call 1-800-845-8820
www.bobbin.com

Brother International *
See your local Brother dealer.
Call 1-800-422-7684 for a dealer near you.
www.brother.com
www.brothermall.com

Brother Embroidery Systems *
Call 1-800-432-3532
www.brother.com

Bubbles Menagerie
www.sew-bubbles.com
www.buzztools.com

Building Blocks
Call 1-888-436-5895
www.bldg-blocks.com

Buzz Tools *
See your local sewing & embroidery dealer.
Call 1-800-850-2899 for dealer near you.
www.buzztools.com

Cactus Punch *
See your local sewing & embroidery dealer.
Call 1-520-622-8460 for a dealer near you.
www.cactuspunch.com

Coats & Clark *
See your local sewing & embroidery dealer.
www.coatsandclark.com

Clotilde
Call 1-800-772-2891
www.clotilde.com

Criswell Embroidery & Design
See your local sewing & embroidery dealer.
Call 1-800-308-5442
www.k-lace.com

***Creative Machine Embroidery* Magazine** *
Subscription Information
Call 1-800-677-5212
www.cmemag.com

Dakota Collectibles *
Call 1-800-331-3160
www.dakotacollectibles.com

***Designs in Machine Embroidery* Magazine**
Subscription Information
Call 1-888-SEW-0555
www.dzgns.com

DMC *
See your local sewing & embroidery dealer.
Call 1-973-589-0606 for a dealer near you.
www.dmc-usa.com

Doumar Products
See your local hardware store.
Call 1-800-289-8638
www.un-du.com

DragonThreads
Call 1-614-267-2914
www.dragonthreads.com

Elna USA *
See your local Elna dealer.
Call 1-800-848-3562 for a dealer near you.
www.elnausa.com

Emblematic USA *
Call 1-800-878-1235
www.emblematicusa.com

Embroideryarts *
See your local sewing & embroidery dealer.
Call 1-888-238-1372 for a dealer near you.
www.embroideryarts.com

***Embroidery Business* News**
Subscription Information
Call 1-480-990-1101
www.ebnmag.com

***Embroidery Enthusiast* Magazine**
Subscription Information
Call 1-800-944-1144 ext 1819
www.homesewing.com

Embroidery/Monogram Business
Subscription Information
Call 847-647-7987
www.embmag.com

Embroidery Resource (The)
www.embroideryresource.com

Embroidery Software Protection Coalition
Call 1-888-921-5732
www.embroideryprotection.org

Embroidery Trade Association
Call 1-800-727-3014
www.eta.mfi.com

Fabric Loft of New England *
Call 1-860-365-0102
www.fabricloft.com

5T's Embroidery Supply
Call 1-800-466-7945
www.5ts.com

Floriani
Call 1-661-822-3234
www.floriani.com

Ghee's *
Call 1-318-226-1701
www.ghees.com

Gingher *
Call 1-800-446-4437
See your local sewing & embroidery dealer.
www.gingher.com

Great Notions
Call 1-800-528-8305
www.greatnotions.com

Gutermann *
See your local sewing & embroidery dealer.
Call 1-888-488-3762 for a dealer near you.
www.gutermann-us.com

Havel's Incorporated
Call 1-800-638-4770
www.havelsinc.com

Herrschners
Call 1-800-328-3894
www.threadsnow.com

Hirsch International
Call 1-800-394-4426
www.hirschintl.com

Hobby Ware, Inc. *
Call 1-800-768-6257
www.hobbyware.com

Home Sewing Association
Call 1-212-714-1633
www.sewing.org

Hoop-It-All *
See your local sewing & embroidery dealer.
Call 1-800-947-4911 for a dealer near you.
www.hoopitall.com

Horn of America
See your local sewing & embroidery dealer.
Call 1-800-882-8845
www.hornofamerica.com

HTC *
See your local sewing & embroidery dealer.
Call 1-888-618-2555 for a dealer near you.
www.htc-inc.net

Hugo's Amazing Tape
See your local sewing & embroidery dealer.
Call 1-323-727-1231
www.getcreativeshow.com/amazingtape.htm

Hummingbird House
See your local embroidery or needlework dealer.
Call 1-760-771-1545 for a dealer near you.
www.hummingbirdhouse.net

Husqvarna/Viking *
See Viking Sewing Machines Inc.

***Impressions* Magazine**
Subscription Information
Call 1-800-527-0207
www.impressionsmag.com

Janome America *
See your local Janome dealer.
Call 1-800-631-0183 for a dealer near you.
www.janome.com

June Tailor *
See your local sewing & embroidery dealer.
Call 1-800-844-5400 for a dealer near you.
www.junetailor.com

KMAC Embroidery
Call 1-508-478-9526
www.ragwool.com

Kenmore
See your local Sears store
Call 1-847-758-0900
www.sears.com

Linda Crone Creations
Call 1-815-654-9601
www.lindacronecreations.com

Madeira USA *
See your local sewing & embroidery dealer.
Call 1-800-225-3001 for a dealer near you.
www.madeirausa.com

Malden Mills Retail Store
Call 1-877-289-7652
www.maldenmillsstore.com

Martha Pullen Co.
Call 1-800-547-4176
www.marthapullen.com

Mary's Productions
Call 1-218-229-2804
www.marymulari.com

Melco Embroidery Systems
Call 1-800-877-4272
www.melco.com

Mountainland Manufacturing *
See your local sewing & embroidery dealer.
Call 1-801-636-3887 for a dealer near you.

Nancy's Notions
Call 1-800-833-0690
www.nancysnotions.com

National Embroidery Supply
Call 1-800-211-2044
www.nebsales.com

National Network of Embroidery Professionals
Call 1-800-866-7396
www.nnep.net

Oklahoma Embroidery Supply & Design (OESD) *
See your local Bernina dealer.
See your local sewing & embroidery dealer.
Call 1-800-580-8885
www.oesd.com
www.embroideryonline.com

Pantograms
Call 1-800-872-1555
www.pantograms.com

Paper Creations *
See your local embroidery & paper products dealer.
Call 1-888-734-6871
www.papercreations.com

PD Sixty Distributors *
See your local sewing & embroidery dealer.
Call 1-800-964-9815 for a dealer near you.

Pellon *
See your local sewing & embroidery dealer.
www.nonwovens-group.com

Peggy's Stitch Eraser *
See your local sewing & embroidery dealer.
Call 1-800-428-4886

Perfect Hooper (The) *
Call 1-800-525-9834
www.theperfecthooper.com

Pfaff American Sales Corp. *
See your local Pfaff dealer.
Call 1-800-997-3233 for a dealer near you.
www.pfaff-us-cda.com

Pres-On Corp.
See your local craft supply dealer.
Call 1-800-323-1744
www.pres-on.com

Robison-Anton *
See your local sewing & embroidery dealer.
Call 1-800-932-0250
www.robison-anton.com

SCS USA
Call 1-800-547-8025

Sew Baby! *
Call 1-800-249-1907
www.sewbaby.com

Sew Beautiful
Subscription Information
Call 1-800-547-4176
www.marthapullen.com

Sew News **Magazine** *
Subscription Information
Call 1-800-289-6397
www.sewnews.com

Sew Special Sew Simple Hooper *
See your local sewing & embroidery dealer.
Call 1-812-359-4180
www.sewsimplehooper.com

Sew Tote Ltd.
Call 1-805-773-1923
www.sewtote.com

Simplicity
Call 1-800-553-5332
www.simplictysewing.com

Singer Company *
See your local Singer dealer.
Call 1-800-474-6437 for a dealer near you.
www.singerco.com

Snap Source, The
See your local sewing & fabric dealer.
Call 1-800-725-4600
www.snapsource.com

SolarActive
See your local sewing & embroidery dealer.
Call 1-818-996-8690 for a dealer near you.
www.solaractiveintl.com

Speed Stitch
Call 1-800-874-4115
www.speedstitch.com

Stitch Shop Embroidery Digitizing
Call 1-770-270-5767
www.needleheads.com

***Stitches* Magazine**
Subscription information
Call 1-800-441-0294
www.stitches.com

Sudberry House *
See your local sewing & embroidery dealer.
Call 1-860-739-6951
www.machinecrossstitch.com
www.sudberry.com

Sulky of America *
See your local sewing & embroidery dealer.
Call 1-800-874-4115 for a dealer near you.
www.sulky.com

Superior Threads *
See your local sewing & embroidery dealer.
Call 1-800-499-1777 for a dealer near you.
www.superiorthreads.com

Suzanne Hinshaw, Inc.
Call 1-407-323-8706
www.suzannehinshaw.com

SWF America
Call 1-800-456-3727
www.mesadist.com
Call 1-877-793-3278
www.swfeast.com
Call 1-800-235-3909
www.ctcemb.com

Sylvia Design Sewing Furniture
See your local sewing & embroidery dealer.
Call 1-800-428-2804 for a dealer near you.
www.sylviadesign.com

Tacony *
See your local Baby Lock or Elna dealer.
Call 1-800-298-8817 for a dealer near you.
www.tacony.com

Tajima-West
Call 1-800-989-7535

ThreadPro
Call 1-888-355-7646
www.threadpro.com

***Threads* Magazine**
Call 1-800-888-8286
www.threadsmagazine.com

Tina's Crosstitch Designs
Call 1-800-237-0137
Access code 37
www.tinascrossstich.com

***Total Embellishment* Newsletter**
Subscription Information
142 Braewick Rd.
Salt Lake City, UT 84103
stchsafe@aol.com

Tristian Embroidery Supplies (Canada) *
Call 1-800-847-3230
www.tristan.bc.ca

Uncommon Thread
Call 1-877-294-5427
www.uncommonthread.com

Vermillion Stitchery
Call 1-949-452-0155
www.vsccs.com

Viking Sewing Machines Inc. *
See your local Husqvarna/Viking dealer.
Call 1-800-358-0001 for a dealer near you.
www.husqvarnaviking.com

Web of Thread
Call 1-800-955-8185
www.webofthread.com

YLI *
See your local sewing & embroidery dealer.
Call 1-800-296-8139 for a dealer near you.
www.ylicorp.com

Recommended Reading

101 Ideas for Machine Embroidery, Country Stitches, 1997

ABC's of Embroidery by Machine, Martha Sheriff & Susan Beck, Bernina of America, 1999

Accessories with Style, Mary Mulari, Krause Publications, 2001

Adventures with Polarfleece, Nancy Cornwell, Krause Publications, 1997

Appliqués with Style, Mary Mulari, Krause Publications, 1998

Complete Book of Machine Embroidery (The), Robbie & Tony Fanning, Chilton, 1986

Creating Textures with Textiles, Linda McGehee, Krause Publications, 1998

Embroidery Embellishments by Machine, Viking Sewing Machine Co., 2000

Fabric Landscapes by Machine, Linda Crone, Krause Publications, 2000

Garments with Style, Mary Mulari, Krause Publications, 1995

Hand Sewn by Machine, Marie Duncan & Betty Farrell, Krause Publications, 1999

It's a Snap!, Jeanine Twigg, Krause Publications, 1998

Kaye Wood's New Strip Cut Quilts, Kay Wood, Krause Publications, 2001

More Polarfleece Adventures, Nancy Cornwell, Krause Publications, 1999

Sew a Beautiful Home, Sally Cowan, Krause Publications, 2000

Sew-It-Yourself Home Décor, Coetzee, Karen & Rene Bergh, Krause Publications, 2000

Simply Sensational Bags, Linda McGehee, Krause Publications, 2000

Sulky Secrets to Successful Quilting!, Joyce Drexler, Sulky of America, 1998

Sulky Secrets to Successful Stabilizing!, Joyce Drexler, Sulky of America, 1999

Techniques of Japanese Embroidery (The), Shuji Tamura, Krause Publications, 1998

Ultimate Rubber Stamping Technique Book (The), Gail Green, Krause Publications, 1999

CD Instructions

To use the designs on the disk, insert the CD into a computer. On a Macintosh, simply download the designs, following the instructions in the ReadMe file. On a PC, an installation page will automatically load onto the screen. From this page, select "Load Designs" and follow the instructions on each screen to install the designs onto the hard-drive of your computer. Be sure to load the designs in your brand-specific embroidery machine's format. Once the designs are on the computer, transfer the designs to the embroidery machine following the manufacturer's instructions for your embroidery equipment. For more information, consult your owner's manual or seek advice from the dealer who honors your equipment warranty.